THE

esearch

ssay

**A
GUIDE
TO
ESSAYS
AND
PAPERS**

Hugh Robertson

McGraw-Hill Ryerson Limited

Toronto Montreal New York Auckland Bogotá
Caracas Lisbon London Madrid Mexico Milan New Delhi
Paris San Juan Singapore Sydney Tokyo

THE RESEARCH ESSAY
A Guide to Essays and Papers

THIRD EDITION

ISBN 0-07-551419-2

2 3 4 5 6 7 8 9 10 BBM 4 3 2 1 0 9 8 7 6 5

Printed and bound in Canada

Canadian Cataloguing in Publication Data
Robertson, Hugh, date—
    The research essay: a guide to essays and papers

3rd ed.
Previous eds. published under title: The research essay : a guide to papers, essays, projects.
Includes bibliographical references.
ISBN 0-07-551419-2

1. Report writing.   2. Research.   I. Title.

LB2369.R62 1994   808'.066   C94-931986-4

PUBLISHER: JANICE MATTHEWS
ASSOCIATE EDITOR: CRYSTAL SHORTT
SENIOR SUPERVISING EDITOR: CAROL ALTILIA
COPY EDITOR: GERALDINE KIKUTA
COVER AND INTERIOR DESIGN: MATTHEWS COMMUNICATIONS DESIGN

This book was manufactured in Canada using acid-free and recycled paper.

ACKNOWLEDGEMENTS

A number of people kindly perused the manuscript of *The Research Essay*. I am indebted to the following persons for their instructive comments and suggestions: Professor Aleksandra Bennett, Professor Alan Gillmor, Tony Horava, Dr. Wayne Howell, Frances Montgomery, Alyssa Novick, Jake Selwood, Mike Jones, Ian Andrews, Ludi Habs, Jeanette Jarosz, and John Einarson.

Matthew Labarge was indefatigable in preparing the manuscript. I am especially grateful for his computer expertise and his endless reserve of good humour. I would also like to express my sincere thanks to Crystal Shortt whose editorial skills helped shape *The Research Essay*.

The process described in this guide has been developed and refined over many years of teaching at Ashbury College. To the students, staff, and administration, my grateful thanks for their support over the years.

CONTENTS

INTRODUCTION

Essay writing is a central part of humanities and social sciences courses from secondary school to graduate school. Writing essays is not always an easy task. However, there are procedures to make it less difficult and to transform the process into a stimulating learning experience.

One of the initial problems facing students is the array of terms associated with writing assignments. These terms range from extended essays and research projects to themes and term papers. Writing an essay is not a creative writing assignment nor an exposition of facts. It is neither a narrative chronicle nor a descriptive composition. **An essay has an argument, or point of view, or thesis.** It is your point of view imprinted on an essay (or term paper) that distinguishes it from other types of writing.

The Research Essay takes you step by step through the entire process of writing a formal essay or term paper — from conception to completion. Using a single example, this manual will guide you through launching the essay, locating sources, gathering ideas and information, organizing the material, and composing a thesis or argument. The process described in the manual is the result of many years of teaching students of various ages. It has been tried and tested. It is not a rigid formula but a flexible model that you can adapt to suit your needs. A history topic is used to demonstrate the process, but the method can be used for essays and term papers in most humanities and social sciences disciplines. Although the manual emphasizes the importance of having an argument or thesis, the method can be modified for descriptive and narrative assignments, reports, reviews, examinations, and seminars.

Writing an essay gives you an opportunity to explore ideas, test hypotheses, and exercise critical judgement. In the process you will develop valuable skills: the ability to locate, organize, and communicate information, and to argue successfully. In addition, you will cultivate qualities like initiative, self-reliance, and confidence. These talents are useful not only in school; they are life-skills of great relevance and wide application.

While *The Research Essay* outlines a process by which you can tackle most assignments confidently and provides advice on quotations, citations, style, and format, it is not exhaustive. You may wish to consult the latest editions of one or more of the following manuals for more detailed information on certain aspects of the writing process:

The Chicago Manual of Style.

A Manual for Writers of Term Papers, Theses, and Dissertations by Kate L. Turabian.

Publication Manual of the American Psychological Association.

Tell me, I will forget
Show me, I may remember
Involve me, I will understand
Chinese proverb

RESEARCH

INTRODUCTION

Once the topic is selected, the research phase starts and continues through the preliminary stages of deciding on the focus, searching for sources, defining the purpose, and finally recording information.

It is important to understand the requirements of the assignment from the start. Discuss and clarify the following items with your instructor so that there is no misunderstanding:

- The exact nature of the assignment, such as whether it is an essay, a report, or a seminar.
- The meaning of terms such as "analyze," "discuss," and "evaluate."
- Whether the sources should include both primary and secondary material.
- The citation or documentation procedures required.
- The length of the completed paper. *10 pages*
- The due date and whether there is a penalty for late submission.
- The contents of the introduction and the conclusion.

- Whether illustrations such as statistical tables and graphs should be used.

- Any other relevant matters, such as style (for example, the use of pronouns) and format (for example, whether subheadings are necessary or accepted).

- The criteria for assessment and whether a sample evaluation form is available.

- Specific manuscript requirements, such as a typed final copy as opposed to a handwritten one.

Regular contact with your instructor should be maintained until the paper is completed. Since requirements will vary among instructors, you might consider making a copy of the above list and checking off the various items during discussions with your instructor.

SELECTING THE TOPIC

Your instructor may assign a topic for an essay or may permit you to select one from a list of topics. Occasionally students may be given a free choice of topics. If you are allowed some freedom to select your own topic, choose one that holds interest for you and offers you a challenge, but also one that is manageable in terms of its scope, complexity, and length.

Let us assume you are studying twentieth-century international history and your instructor has asked you to choose the topic for your term paper. After studying the course outline carefully and looking through the textbook, you select "Collective Security in the 1930s" as the broad subject area you wish to investigate. We will use this topic to illustrate the process of researching and writing an essay or term paper.

Discuss your choice of topic with the instructor and clarify the items listed on the previous page. As soon as the due date is established, start planning a schedule for the completion of the various stages of the paper. The stages are explained in the pages ahead. For example, you may wish to spend half the time on the research phase and the other half on the actual writing of the paper. Alternatively, you may decide to spend about one-third of the time on the preliminary research, one-third on recording information, and one-third on the actual writing. If a topic has been assigned, some of the initial stages of the preliminary research will be eliminated and this will influence the scheduling. Develop a schedule that is tailored to **your** needs and routines. Plot a schedule for **each** assignment on a calendar or in your research notebook. Advance planning is critical, since you are unlikely to learn much, derive any satisfaction, or achieve any success if your essay is written in frenzied haste the night before the assignment is due.

NARROWING THE FOCUS

If your instructor has not provided you with a specific issue, your first task is to narrow the topic. Focus on **one** significant issue — an important problem or a major controversy. If you know very little about your topic, it will be necessary to do some preliminary reading to isolate an issue for investigation. Textbooks, general surveys, and reference books such as encyclopedias, atlases, and dictionaries are useful for this exploratory reading.[1] Not all dictionaries are language publications. For example, there are biographical dictionaries and historical dictionaries. The library catalogue and indexes at the back of books and encyclopedias may provide interesting leads. In addition, you might consult the *Library of Congress Subject Headings* and periodical and newspaper indexes which are explained in the Appendix. Viewing films and television documentaries on your topic could also suggest new ideas.

You can assemble a group of fellow students to brainstorm essay issues and exchange ideas. As you read, think, and brainstorm, look for the major features and aspects of your topic and jot them down in a writing folder or notebook. It is a useful practice to keep a research notebook or an *Ideas and Questions Journal* — an "*I.Q. Journal*" — in which to record ideas, questions, and issues. Instead of listing the issues and features, you could use different diagrammatic techniques when reading and brainstorming. For example, you might sketch the different possibilities in your *I.Q. Journal* as shown in the diagram on the following page.

List as many possibilities in your *I.Q. Journal* as you can from your reading and brainstorming. Think carefully about your list of issues before deciding on one. **Narrowing the topic is a crucial stage in the process because the issue you select will provide the focus for your investigation.** It is important to devote your attention to a manageable aspect that is not too big and not too small. If an issue is too narrow, there may be insufficient source material, and if it is too broad, it risks becoming a superficial survey.

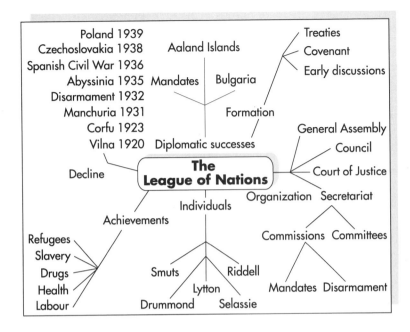

You should also avoid issues that lend themselves to a largely narrative, descriptive, or biographical approach. Controversial issues produce provocative essays because they are usually widely written about and they provide an opportunity to test conflicting interpretations, perspectives, and values. It is also a good idea to have one or two backup issues listed in your *I.Q. Journal* in case you run into difficulties with your first choice.

Frequently, this narrowing or focusing process will involve more than one stage. If you had chosen "Collective Security in the 1930s" as your topic, you might decide to focus on the League of Nations and then discover that it is still too broad an aspect for study. This could lead you to narrow the topic further to examine the inability of the League to maintain international stability in the 1930s.

Imagine that your topic is a scene you are viewing through a pair of wide-angle binoculars. Then you change to a zoom-lens and zoom in closer until your subject is manageable and focused. You can always zoom out again to check perspective and context.[2]

SEARCHING FOR SOURCES

Once you have decided on a specific focus for your research, the next step is to compile a list of potential sources of information.* It is important to determine as soon as possible whether there are sufficient sources available on your issue. If not, you will have to substitute your second choice.

Libraries can appear overwhelming, but there is no need to panic. If introductory tours are available, start by signing up for a tour of your library and later wander around on your own, familiarizing yourself with the layout. Many libraries provide handouts on everything from regulations to lists of reference materials. Develop a collection of these information sheets and read them carefully. Approach the library staff if you have difficulties. They are the specialists with the expertise to answer your questions. Their advice and suggestions will save hours of your time.

A great variety of source material is available today and most libraries have a wide array of searching techniques to trace this material. To avoid diverting you from the research process by describing these techniques here, they have been placed in the Appendix. Read pages 91–99 carefully. Do not be intimidated by the range of research resources. You are likely to use only a few of these techniques initially. As you do research assignments during your high-school and undergraduate years, try to familiarize yourself with as many of these resources as possible. Test them out in your library: hands-on, practical experience is a far better teacher than a manual. Knowing which resources exist in your research field will not only save time but will allow you to build a wide-ranging list of sources. And, of course, a knowledge of the various research aids will make it easier for you to write subsequent essays and papers.

---

* You may wish to define more precisely the purpose of your assignment before searching for sources. If so, merely reverse the next two stages, "Searching for Sources" and "Defining the Purpose." If your instructor has assigned a topic and spelled out the purpose then definitely reverse these stages.

As you work through the research aids, you will be looking for sources relevant to your issue or problem — the focus of your research. This preliminary list of sources is known as your Working Bibliography. At this stage you are simply listing the titles and details of publication of your sources: there is no need to locate and assemble the material.

Enter all the publication details for each source accurately, because these details will be required for the final bibliography. If you do this conscientiously, there will be no need to check the sources again and waste valuable time. There is no need to write up these details in their final format at this stage. You will notice in our examples on the following two pages that we have used different procedures on the index cards and in the notepaper examples. We have followed the procedures of *The Chicago Manual of Style* in the notepaper examples and the procedures of the *American Psychological Association* (APA) on the index cards. These procedures are explained on pages 65–88. Frequently, your instructor will indicate the system that you are expected to use.

Although the final bibliography is listed alphabetically, do not attempt at this stage to place your preliminary sources in alphabetical order. Concentrate on finding as many sources as possible, and just list the publication details accurately.

There are three recommended methods of building the Working Bibliography: you can use standard notepaper, index cards, or a computer. The bibliographic information can be listed in exactly the same way in all three methods. Choose the method that best suits your needs.

Notepaper Method

As you discover potential sources of information in your searching, list them on standard notepaper and fill in all the essential bibliographic details as follows:

	Working Bibliography
LNLT	Northedge, F.S. The League of Nations: Its Life and Times, 1920–1946. Leicester: Leicester University Press, 1986. Public Library, JX 1975.N78.
CSPM	Egerton, George W. "Collective Security as Political Myth: Liberal Internationalism and the League of Nations in Politics and History." International Historical Review 5 (1983): 496–524. University Library. SER: H1.15.

- Continue listing all your sources in this manner.

- The codes, LNLT and CSPM, represent shortened forms of the titles. Codes are used to identify sources during the research. Develop your own coding system if you prefer.

- Enter the call number and the library where the source is located.

Index Card Method

As you discover potential sources of information in your searching, list them on separate cards and fill in all the essential bibliographic details as follows:

LNLT

Northedge, F.S. (1986). The League of Nations: Its life and times, 1920–1946. Leicester: Leicester University Press.
Public Library. JX 1975.N78.

CSPM

Egerton, George W. (1983). Collective security as political myth: Liberal internationalism and the League of Nations in politics and history. International Historical Review, 5, 496–524.
University Library. SER: H1.15.

- Continue listing all your sources on separate cards in this manner.

- The codes, LNLT and CSPM, represent shortened forms of the titles. Codes are used to identify sources during the research. Develop your own coding system if you prefer.

- Enter the call number and the library where the source is located.

Computer Method

Computer technology is transforming researching and writing techniques. You can use computers to search for sources, develop the Working Bibliography, and store the research information.

Using a computer and a modem, you can search library holdings and other databases from your computer through a telephone link. Electronic searching for sources is explained in the Research Aids section of the Appendix. You can either copy the sources manually from the screen onto index cards or notepaper (as explained in the previous two pages) or you can have the computer capture the information into a Working Bibliography file and print it later.

You could also search manually for your sources in the various research aids and then, using a portable computer and a word processing program, you can set up a Working Bibliography file and enter the publication details as shown on the previous page. Software programs even allow you to create your own electronic index cards if you prefer cards to notepaper for your Working Bibliography.

The range of your sources can dramatically enhance the quality of your essays. When building your Working Bibliography try to balance books and articles, print and nonprint sources, old and new material, conservative and radical interpretations, and primary and secondary information.

To expand the diversity of your sources you can classify them in groups such as Books, Articles (popular magazines, scholarly journals, and newspapers), General (neither book nor article, such as an atlas), Audio-Visual, and Primary. You can then use different-coloured index cards, for example, blue for books and yellow for articles, to identify the different categories of sources. Enter the details as shown on page 11. If you are using notepaper for your Working Bibliography, you can classify your sources in a similar way by devoting a separate page to each category. Simply head your pages Books, Articles, General, and so forth, and write in the source details as shown on page 10.

If you are searching electronically, you can print out your sources and cut and paste them onto coloured cards or pages of notepaper. Alternatively, you can copy the sources to disk instead of printing them. Then you can create separate files for the different categories such as Books and Articles and transfer the sources to the respective files. You can print them later if necessary.

You may wish to devise your own set of classified headings to extend the range of your sources. There is a rich vein of source material available today and a variety of techniques to trace the material. Combine tradition, technology, and tenacity in combing the various research aids for sources. Careful use of these aids, and frequent practice, will save you hours of frustrated searching, and you will be surprised at the quantity of information you can assemble on almost any topic. You will undoubtedly experience obstacles and frustrations in digging for material, but do not give up: the persistent researcher is invariably rewarded.

Once you have assured yourself that there are adequate sources of information available, move to the next stage. The length of your Working Bibliography will be determined either by the nature of the assignment or by the instructor. For most high-school and undergraduate papers, a *preliminary* list of 10 to 20 sources should be adequate. However, if there are insufficient sources, despite intensive searching, you will have to select another issue from the backup list in your *I.Q. Journal.* **Make the change at this early stage.** It is very frustrating to discover as the deadline approaches that there are insufficient sources to build a paper. By determining the extent of potential sources at this stage you will avoid the agony of having to find another issue and start again with the deadline looming.

Compilation of the Working Bibliography does not stop at this stage it is an ongoing process. You will probably keep adding useful sources to your list throughout the research.

DEFINING THE PURPOSE

Once you have narrowed your topic to an important issue and established that there are sufficient sources of information, the next step is to define more clearly the direction of your research. You can give a firm sense of direction to your essay by launching it with an incisive and challenging **research question.** This is a crucial stage because the question spells out your **purpose.** Your quest is in the question.

The nature of the question also defines the scope and focus of the essay and influences its length. If you are expected to produce a short paper, do not get carried away and pose a question that would produce a book. The question must be clear, precise, and free of ambiguities. If it has these qualities, it will give direction and purpose to the assignment. Your sole task is to answer the question. **The answer will form your thesis, argument, or point of view.**

Since your purpose is to develop a thesis or argument, you should avoid questions that lead to biographical, narrative, or descriptive answers such as "Who was Grey Owl?" or "What are the different types of Native Art?" Also, do not pose questions of a speculative or hypothetical nature such as "Could Germany have won the Second World War?" There can be no conclusive answers to conjectures of this nature. Take care to avoid questions that may be based on unfounded assumptions such as "Why was Lenin a successful leader?" The assumption here is that Lenin was a successful leader, and that might not turn out to be the consensus view of your sources. It would be safer to rephrase the question in an open-ended way as follows: "How effective was Lenin as a leader?"

Always try to pose a **single, challenging question** that demands analysis and argument — a question that can be stated briefly and succinctly in just one sentence. Avoid compound or multiple questions because they usually create confusion. "Why" questions such as "Why did the U.S.A. declare war in 1917?" work well because they lend themselves to clear, structured answers and give a well-defined direction and focus to your investigation.

If you have difficulty in formulating a good question, it may be necessary to do additional reading on the issue you selected. Frequently, in searching for sources for your Working Bibliography, you will discover interesting ideas, perspectives, and questions simply from titles and abstracts in the different indexes. Further brainstorming sessions with fellow students can help expand your range of options. Gather as many potential research questions as possible and note them in your *I.Q. Journal*. Think carefully before making your final decision, and then check with your instructor to ensure that the question is acceptable and appropriately phrased.

Let us return to our example, the inability of the League of Nations to maintain international stability in the 1930s. Assuming that our interest is in the reasons underlying the diplomatic problems that plagued the League, we might formulate the research question as follows: "Why did the League of Nations fail to maintain international stability in the 1930s?" The direction of the essay is clearly set. **Your task is to answer the question — that is the sole purpose of the assignment. Your answer will take the form of a thesis, argument, or point of view.**

Some manuals suggest initiating the research by proposing a hypothesis or tentative theory. The difficulty with this approach is that you must have the background knowledge to suggest a sound hypothesis as a starting point. Furthermore, there is the temptation to select material to support your position, while rejecting material that runs counter to it.[*] Launching your essay with a precise question such as "Why did the League of Nations fail to maintain international stability in the 1930s?" opens up a wider range of possibilities than starting from a fixed position such as "The League of Nations failed because of ineffective leadership." It might be useful to remember Sherlock Holmes' advice: never theorize in advance of the facts.

---

[*] Certain types of assignments, especially those involving statistical data, do lend themselves to the formulation and testing of a hypothesis. However, avoid starting with an "educated guess" and then selecting information "to prove the thesis." It is dishonest to select material that supports a predetermined position, while rejecting information that runs counter to it.

PREPARATORY READING

Once you have defined the purpose of your research and have determined that there are sufficient sources available, you need to develop a better understanding of the focus of your investigation. You will have done some exploratory and preliminary reading in narrowing your topic and defining the purpose. In addition to the general sources you used earlier, such as textbooks, encyclopedias, and dictionaries, you might locate a few of the more specific sources from your Working Bibliography and read them quickly. Reading the specific source material beforehand gives you an idea of the overall content before you start recording information and enables you to determine whether the sources have any merit.

The investment of your time in the preparatory reading is well worth it because you are "preparing" yourself for an important stage of the research: recording information and ideas that you need to develop your thesis or argument. The preparatory reading will provide you with the background knowledge that you can use to develop perceptive questions, and it will provide you with a basis for judging what is relevant and important in the answers. Much of the reading, brainstorming, and even some of your research notes never appear in the final copy. But like the nine-tenths of an iceberg that is below the surface of the water, they are part of the invisible foundations that keep the essay afloat.

You are not doing formal research at this stage; you are doing the preparatory reading to acquaint yourself with the focus of your investigation. **While you are reading, keep the question or purpose uppermost in your mind.** Elements of an argument or thesis might start to emerge. Likewise a tentative structure for the essay might start to appear. * Note these responses and ideas in your *I.Q. Journal.* You might even discover a more interesting and challenging purpose than your original choice. Do not hesitate to change direction — providing the sources in your Working Bibliography are appropriate — and formulate another research question. Do it now, not later. Discuss any changes with your instructor.

---

* Some students prefer to structure a Working Outline in advance and use it as the framework for recording their information. If you wish to use a Working Outline for your research see pages 100–104 in the Appendix.

RECORDING INFORMATION AND IDEAS

Armed with a thorough understanding of your subject from your preparatory reading, a substantial list of sources, and an incisive question, you are now ready to start analyzing your material and recording the relevant information and ideas. The preliminary research is necessary: there are no shortcuts.

First you have to locate your sources. Do not panic if you cannot find all the sources in your Working Bibliography, as it is unlikely that they will all be available in your community libraries. That is why you originally listed more sources in your Working Bibliography than you really needed. The number of sources that you actually use may be determined by the instructor, by the scope of the essay, or by the length of the sources themselves. You should be able to complete a high-school or undergraduate paper with between 7 and 12 sources. As you locate a source, note the library and catalogue number (if you have not done so already) in your Working Bibliography so that you can find it again easily if necessary. Check off each source once you have finished using it to record information.

LNLT

Northedge, F.S. (1986). The League of Nations: Its life and times, 1920–1946. Leicester: Leicester University Press.

Public Library JX 1975.N78.   ✓

Using a variety of source material will improve your essay. A source may be biased, unbalanced, or even erroneous. By consulting a number of sources, you gain access to a wider range of interpretations and information. Frequently you will encounter conflicting information, and a wider range of sources will often enable you to corroborate (or reject) controversial information.

Primary sources are original records and data and include the accounts of eyewitnesses, personal memoirs and recollections, literary works, and official documents. Primary material may be in published form such as the report of a journalist, an autobiography, or a government document such as an international treaty. Primary information is often unpublished such as letters, diaries, and taped speeches. Much primary material is in nonprint form such as customs, traditions, legends, and folklore. Inscriptions on old buildings, archaeological artifacts, and even human and animal remains constitute primary material. Primary sources include original films, photographs, and works of art, and also statistical data such as election results and population changes. You can collect your own primary material by interviewing eyewitnesses and by conducting surveys and fieldwork exercises.

A major problem facing researchers when handling primary material is the authenticity of their sources and the credibility of their evidence. Is a document perhaps a forgery, and if not, how reliable is the information? Is it fact, or is it fiction? Does a diarist have concealed motives? How trustworthy is the autobiography of a prominent person? How accurate are the statistics, or has a photograph been reconstructed? Has a painting been forged, or how genuine is an artifact? Verifying (determining authenticity) and evaluating (determining reliability) evidence is an important facet of research. Since students may not have the time or the expertise to engage in critical testing of primary sources, it may be necessary to consult teachers, professors, librarians, and archivists.

Secondary sources are based on primary material. They are written at a later date than the primary source on which they are based and from which they draw their conclusions. Secondary sources present another person's evaluation of the primary material, and they usually develop an argument or point of view.

Most of your sources will probably be secondary sources representing other writers' interpretations in books and articles. There are means of determining the reliability of secondary sources. For example, how well known is the author, or how reputable is the publishing company? Is the article published in a respected journal? How recently was it published? How frequently is the author cited in other sources? Is the source based on primary material or just on secondary sources? Is the source based on circumstantial evidence or unfounded assumptions? Does the author treat the subject fairly? Are the arguments well supported with relevant evidence? Are both sides of the issue examined? Does the author use slanted language? You might also consult a review of the book to ascertain its reliability. Questions of this type will help you determine the quality of your sources.[3]

Research in the humanities and social sciences is not a mechanical gathering of "facts." It is a complex process requiring insight, thought, and creative imagination. You have to dissect the material and evaluate interpretations and judgements as you search for an answer to your research question. Read critically: do not accept ideas and interpretations blindly. Be skeptical: read between the lines and beyond the print. Question continuously as you read, and examine carefully the arguments and hypotheses of the authors. **Raise your own stimulating and challenging questions; they can yield surprising new insights.**

The evidence that you unearth in your sources will fall into two broad categories:

- Factual information or data.

- Ideas, judgements, inferences, theories, and opinions of other writers and scholars.

Part of your task as a researcher is to determine whether a piece of evidence is established fact or personal opinion.

Remember that your task is to develop a thoughtful and convincing answer to your research question. The answer will form your thesis, argument, or point of view. Since you cannot remember everything you read, a systematic method of recording ideas and information is essential. **It is impossible to develop a good essay without an organized collection of notes.** Recording your information is much more effective than trying to remember it.

Research involves analyzing, selecting, and recording information and ideas. Analysis means breaking something down into smaller parts. As you read through your sources, examine the material carefully and extract the important ideas and information that are relevant to your research question. Once you have isolated the relevant details and identified the key ideas, you record them (the smaller parts) in your research notes. Remember that **your research question guides your research**: the question directs the analysis, the selection, and the recording of the information.

Take special care in the way you select your notes — to look for information just to "prove" a preconceived position is unethical. You should consider all sides of your question and **record all relevant information** whether it supports or contradicts your personal position on the issue that you are investigating.

Recorded notes can take different forms:

- Direct quotations.

- Personal ideas, insights, comments, and questions.

- Paraphrasing information and ideas.

- Summarizing information and ideas.

Itemized below are some suggestions to assist you in compiling your research notes:

- If possible, read your sources before recording information and ideas from them.

- Be concise, clear, and accurate.

- Add your own ideas and questions; do not just paraphrase and summarize what you read.

- If you develop your own shorthand system for notemaking, ensure that your abbreviations and symbols will make sense to you later.

- Use your own words where possible.

- Restrict the number of direct quotations.

- Transcribe direct quotations carefully.

- Record the essential information so that you do not have to consult the sources again.

- Indicate whether a piece of evidence is established fact or subjective opinion.

- Material may be interesting and it may be true, but ask yourself if it is relevant to your question or purpose.

- Plagiarism is the unacknowledged use of someone else's ideas. Plagiarism is a serious academic offence. Identifying the sources of all your notes can help you avoid charges of plagiarism.

There are three ways that you can record information and ideas. You can use standard notepaper, index cards, or a computer. Whichever method you use, the notemaking techniques that are described in detail under "Notepaper" remain basically the same. Therefore, you should read the Notepaper section carefully, even if you are using index cards or a computer, since the notemaking techniques are not repeated in those sections.

Notepaper Method

Set up your notepaper recording system by ruling a right-hand margin of approximately 3 cm **on the front side of the page only**. Prepare a number of pages in advance so that you have a supply of notepaper for your research notes.

If you were doing the League of Nations essay, you would take one of your available sources, for example, *The League of Nations: Its Life and Times, 1920–1946* by F.S. Northedge, and start looking specifically for information relevant to the research question. On page 52 of that book there is reference to the limited power of the League, and since this point is relevant to your question, you would record it in the centre column of your notepaper as shown in the example on the following page.

You must identify the source of the note in case you need to refer to it for further details or need to acknowledge the source in a documentary note. It is not necessary to record all the publication details (author, title, publisher, year) again for each note. Simply use the code that stands for a shortened form of the title. For example, *The League of Nations: Its Life and Times, 1920–1946* becomes LNLT as shown on pages 10, 11, and 17. In addition to the source, you must also indicate the page reference for the information. Therefore, LNLT 52 indicates that the information is from page 52 in *The League of Nations: Its Life and Times, 1920–1946*, as illustrated in the example on the following page.

Reflect on what you have done:

- You have discovered relevant information pertaining to the research question.

- You have recorded it in note form.

- You have indicated the source and page number.

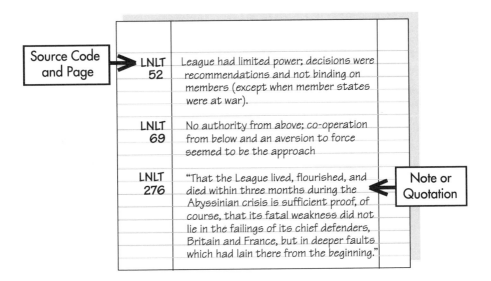

Continue reading through LNLT looking for information and ideas relevant to the research question. On page 69, there is reference to the authority of the League. In similar fashion to the first note, you record the information in the centre column and identify the source by its code and page number in the left-hand margin. Nothing is written in the right-hand margin at this stage. Leave a line between each note so that they can be separated later.

On page 276, there is mention of the Abyssinian crisis, and you may decide to note the information verbatim in case it is needed as a quotation. Record it accurately and use quotation marks to indicate that it is a quotation and not a summary or a paraphrased note. The source code and page are recorded as usual. You may wish to consult section V on Quotations before starting your research.

Work through your first source questioning, analyzing, selecting, and recording the relevant information. Do not record information just because it is "interesting." Does the information help answer the research question? That must always be your criterion. Use the table of contents and index in each book so that you can save time by focusing just on the pertinent pages. Once you have filled your first page of notepaper, continue on another page. **Do not write on the reverse side of the page** because these notes will be separated later.

When you have completed your first source, check it in your Working Bibliography (see page 17) and move to the next available source — George Egerton's article, coded CSPM, for example. It is not necessary to start a new page of notepaper for each source. On page 513 of article CSPM, you find mention of the nature of support for collective security, and you summarize the point in your notes and identify the source as shown below. Read through the source isolating the relevant information and recording it in the manner described.

CPSM 513	Many supporters of collective security were idealists who opposed military sanctions to curb aggressive states.	

Continue reading all your available sources, searching for information, ideas, and insights relevant to your purpose or question and systematically recording them and identifying the sources on your notepaper.

While you are engaged in your research, you may discover so much information on one aspect that you decide to narrow the focus even further and zoom in closer. For example, you may decide to focus on just the League's role in the Abyssinian crisis. You may even decide on a minor shift of direction and modify your question slightly during the course of the research. **Always consult your instructor before making any major changes.**

Index Card Method

Instead of using notepaper for recording your information, you can use index cards. There are only minor differences between the two methods. Read pages 22–24 carefully because they contain many points about notemaking techniques that are not repeated in this section. You have a choice of three common sizes of index cards. The smallest size card is recommended because each note should be written on a separate index card. The source code and page number are entered as explained earlier. If you were using index cards instead of notepaper to record information from *The League of Nations: Its Life and Times, 1920–1946*, your notes as shown on page 23 would appear as follows:

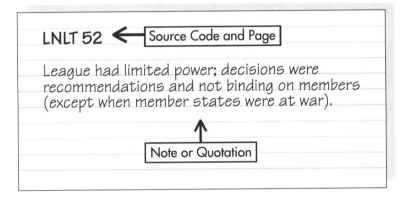

LNLT 276

"That the League lived, flourished, and died within three months during the Abyssinian crisis is sufficient proof, of course, that its fatal weakness did not lie in the failings of its chief defenders, Britain and France, but in deeper faults which had lain there from the beginning."

The only difference is that the notepaper method links the "index cards" together, which many students find convenient. On the other hand, individual index cards are more efficient when you structure and draft your paper, because they can be shuffled into groups.

Once you have completed recording information on separate index cards from LNLT, check it on your Working Bibliography and move to your next source. Work your way through the source, in our example, George Egerton's article coded CSPM, isolating the relevant information and recording it on separate index cards in the manner described.

CSPM 513

Many supporters of collective security were idealists who opposed military sanctions to curb aggressive states.

Continue reading all your available sources searching for information, ideas, and insights relevant to your purpose or question and systematically record them and identify the sources on separate index cards.

Bear these points in mind when you are doing your research on index cards:

- Each card should contain two items:

  1. Source code and page

  2. Note

- Write just one note on each card.

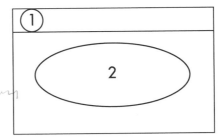

- Use the smallest index cards. It is easier to shape your outlines with small cards, each containing just one major point.

- Your research cards have no special order, so do not number them. They are all independent and each one is identified by its source code and page reference.

- Finish writing a long note on the reverse side of the card rather than continuing on another card.

- Use cards to copy diagrams, graphs, and statistical tables as well.

- Keep separate "date cards" while researching history essays. Creating a chronology or time line will be easy.

- Record your own ideas either on cards or in your *I.Q. Journal.* Use your initials for the source code.

- Do not confuse bibliography cards, which list sources, with research cards, which contain ideas and information.

- You may also use coloured cards to distinguish different types of cards. For example, you might use white cards for research notes, blue cards for sources, and yellow cards for "date cards." (If you colour coded your Working Bibliography cards, do not use coloured cards as suggested here.)

- Use a file box or two-ring card folder to organize your cards.

Computer Method

Recording your ideas and information with a computer is also an option. Modern, portable computers are powerful enough to allow you to work in libraries and archives for extended periods. If you prefer using a computer, you should still read pages 22–27 carefully because they contain many points about notemaking techniques not covered in this section. If you prefer the notepaper method, you can set up a word processor file for all your notes. Remember to code each source and provide the page reference. If you prefer index cards, there are many software packages that will let you write, edit, retrieve, and sort cards on the screen. Make sure, however, that your recorded notes can be "exported" to the word-processing program with which you will write the essay.

Modems and networks are providing quick and easy access to library holdings and other databases. The information in those databases is often in a variety of formats such as text, video, sound, graphics, and photographs. You can browse and "import" information in text or graphic form directly to your note files, but remember the warning about plagiarism and copyright infringement when downloading from electronic sources.

Whatever method you choose to record information and ideas, remember to keep these points in mind:

- Allow enough time in your schedule for recording your information. You need adequate time to read, research, respond, reflect, and record.

- A comprehensive and organized system of notes is essential. It is exceedingly difficult to write an intelligent essay without good notes.

- The process described is not rigid. Modify or adapt it to suit your needs.

- Brainstorm and question continuously as you research and use your I.Q. Journal to list major ideas and insights.

- There is a time to stop digging and start shaping.[4] Learn to impose limits on your research.

PRESENTATION

INTRODUCTION

Now that the research stage has been completed, you can start composing your answer to the question. This is a crucial phase because the **success of your essay hinges on your ability to communicate your answer or argument clearly to the reader**. Clarity of argument is largely dependent upon style and structure. Contrary to what many people think, structure does not suppress creativity; it promotes clear, creative expression.[5] The ABC formula below is a simple and effective model for structuring essays and term papers.

A. INTRODUCTION

B. BODY I ⟶ YOUR
  II   MAIN
  III ⟶ SECTIONS

C. CONCLUSION

Shaping the structure of your essay is your next task. The following section on outlining demonstrates the importance of organization in developing clarity of argument before you start to draft your essay.

29

SHAPING THE OUTLINES

Once you have completed your research, your notes will be organized on notepaper, index cards, or computer. It is difficult to write a final copy straight from these notes. A number of intermediate stages are necessary to ensure quality.

Remember that the purpose of your essay is to develop an answer to your research question, and to articulate it in the form of an argument or thesis. The first step is to create an outline that imposes order on your notes. The method in this manual describes what might be called "conventional outlining." Some students might have alternative organizing systems such as "web-bing," "mapping," or "tree diagramming." It does not matter what you call your system; **it is important to have a system**.

Basic Outline

Reread your notes, keeping your research question uppermost in your mind. Try to isolate the **main factors** around which you can structure an answer. You may even have started listing possible factors in your *I.Q. Journal* during the course of the preparatory reading and the research. In the example on the following page, we have listed the main factors that will be used to develop an answer to our question: "Why did the League of Nations fail to maintain international stability in the 1930s?" This list of main factors is called the Basic Outline.

BASIC OUTLINE

A. INTRODUCTION

B. I   STRUCTURE OF LEAGUE
       II MOTIVES OF MEMBER STATES
       III FAILURE TO RESOLVE CRISES

C. CONCLUSION

There is no magic number of sections in a Basic Outline —
from three to six will handle most questions comfortably. If you
used notepaper for recording your information, separate the
individual notes with scissors (that is why you wrote on one side
of the page only), in effect making "cards" out of them. Read
through the separated notepaper slips carefully and group them
according to the sections of the Basic Outline.

The next step is to number the notepaper slips according
to the sections of the Basic Outline into which they fall. Use
the empty right-hand column to indicate the numbered
section of the Basic Outline. For instance, all notes dealing
with problems associated with the structure of the League of
Nations are labeled I because "Structure of the League" is
section I of the Basic Outline as shown above. It is a good idea
to use paper clips to group the notepaper slips.

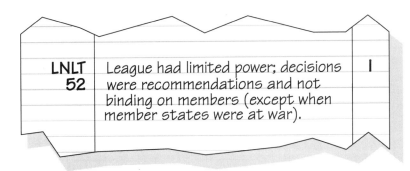

| LNLT 52 | League had limited power; decisions were recommendations and not binding on members (except when member states were at war). | I |

If you used index cards for recording your information, go through your cards in exactly the same way and group and number them according to the sections of the Basic Outline. Arrange your cards in their groups in a file box, a two-ring card folder, or with rubber bands.

```
LNLT 52                                    I

League had limited power;
decisions were recommendations
and not binding on members
(except when member states
were at war).
```

Some notes will not fit into the major sections of the Body or in the Introduction, and they will have to be discarded. Do not be concerned if you cannot use all your notes. The rejected notes are not wasted: they are part of the "invisible foundations" that will support your essay. Forcing all your notes into the essay will clutter it with debris and destroy its clarity.

If you used a computer to record your material, you might find it easier at this stage to print copies of your notes and organize them manually, as described above. If you do not feel this is necessary, you can reorganize your electronic notes according to your outline. If you used a word processor, you can create separate files for each section of the outline and transfer the notes to the appropriate files. If you used specific index card software, it is easy to group your notes in this manner.

Skeleton Outline

The Basic Outline provides the overall structure of your essay. Your research notes are grouped and numbered according to the sections of the Basic Outline. The next step is to read carefully through the notes of each section, looking for the important subsections around which you can shape that section. The advantage of notepaper strips or index cards is that you can take a section at a time and spread the strips or cards on a table. It is easy to move them around and map out the substructure for each section. This stage, containing the main sections with their subsections, is called the Skeleton Outline.

SKELETON OUTLINE

A. INTRODUCTION
1. Background
2. Focus/Problem
3. Question
4. Different interpretations
5. Thesis

B. I STRUCTURE OF LEAGUE
1. Limits to power
2. Problem with mandate
3. Abuse of major powers

II MOTIVES OF MEMBER STATES
1. Lack of idealism
2. "Balance of power" diplomacy
3. Nationalistic ends and propaganda

III FAILURE TO RESOLVE CRISES
1. Manchuria — powerlessness
2. Abyssinia — secret diplomacy
3. Loss of public confidence
4. Inequality of member states

C. CONCLUSION

Point-form Outline

Remember that the purpose of your essay is to develop and substantiate an argument or thesis. In our example, we are not simply describing or chronicling the failure of the League of Nations—we are explaining **why** we believe it failed to maintain international security. **It is your point of view that is stamped on an essay.** Study carefully the ideas, insights, and questions that you jotted down in your *I.Q. Journal* and integrate them as you construct your essay. Aim for a novel and fresh approach in developing an answer to your question.

Judgements, interpretations, and opinions have to be developed and defended by relevant information and sound reasoning if your argument is to be credible and convincing. Evidence comes in many forms: statistics, cases, examples, reasoning, and quotations from authorities. Arguments in some academic disciplines —history and geography for instance—tend to be supported by factual and statistical evidence, while arguments in other disciplines—philosophy and English for instance—more readily find support through reasoning and the critical analysis of abstract ideas.

The Point-form Outline requires you to search through your notes and isolate the supporting detail for each section under the substructure of the Skeleton Outline. This should not be a lengthy process because you already have a good overall knowledge of the contents of your notes and a clear idea of the direction your essay is taking. However, this stage does require further selection. Choose the essential information that is directly relevant to the point of view that you are developing. Be ruthless and reject the irrelevant notes.

There is rarely a need for a Conclusion in the initial drafting stages because new information should not be included in the concluding section. However, if you have special points that you wish to mention in the Conclusion then add them to the outlines. The contents of the Conclusion are explained on page 48.

Use as few words as possible in the Point-form Outline; do not rewrite your notes. You can always refer to your research notes to check details when writing your rough draft. Since the order of the main sections may change in the final copy, it is advisable to devote a separate page to each major section in the Point-form Outline. It is then easy to reorganize the sections in the desired order when drafting the next stage. Notepaper is recommended for the detailed outlines, or alternatively large index cards, as there is insufficient space on the small cards.

We have taken section III of the body to illustrate the Point-form Outline.

POINT-FORM OUTLINE

B. III FAILURE TO RESOLVE CRISES

1. Manchuria (powerlessness of League)
   — Western policy of non-recognition
   — unwilling to use force against Japan
   — Japan leaves League

2. Abyssinia (secret diplomacy)
   — need for Italian support
   — reluctance to impose oil embargo
   — Hoare–Laval plan

3. Loss of public confidence
   — peace ballot shows support
   — disillusionment after Hoare–Laval

4. Inequality of member states
   — lack of racial equality clause
   — League primarily serving Europe

If you have been using a computer, look through your electronic notes isolating the subsections of the Skeleton Outline and the supporting detail of the Point-form Outline. Most word processors allow you to split your screen into "windows," enabling you to develop your outline in one window while viewing your notes in another window. Most word processing programs also have an Outline function built in. This function will automatically number the sections and subsections as you go along, making it easy for you to create outlines.

Developing the Skeleton and Point-form Outlines is not excessively time-consuming, and the payoff lies in having a clear structure for paragraphing and weaving the rough draft. It also enables you to determine if there are any weak spots in the argument. For instance, a Point-form Outline might show you that one of your main sections contains insufficient material to support your thesis and that it might be better to merge this with another section or eliminate it.

Notice in the diagram below how the expansion of B. III is shown at each outline stage. Clarity of argument is a function of both style and structure. In shaping your outlines you will have created the structure. **Style is the mortar that will hold the essay together.** Style is covered in section VI.

Basic Outline	Skeleton Outline	Point-form Outline
B. III Failure to Resolve Crises	III Failure to Resolve Crises 1. Manchuria (powerlessness) 2. Abyssinia (secret diplomacy) 3. Loss of public confidence 4. Inequality of member states	III Failure to Resolve Crises 1. Manchuria (powerlessness) — Western policy of non-recognition — unwilling to use force against Japan — Japan leaves League 2. Abyssinia (secret diplomacy) — need for Italian support — reluctance to impose oil embargo — Hoare–Laval plan 3. Loss of public confidence — peace ballot shows support — disillusionment after Hoare–Laval 4. Inequality of member states — lack of racial equality clause — League primarily serving Europe

Bias, Subjectivity, and Selection

The research process has taken you from the initial launching stages to analyzing, selecting, and recording the relevant information and ideas. You then set about synthesizing and refining your answer. The whole process (research and synthesis) is influenced by your unique view of the world.

Our subjective worldview has been to a great extent individually shaped by our life experiences. We view the past and the present through the prism of these experiences. Family, friends, institutions, and the values of society have all left their imprint. This socialization process influences the selection of our subject, the nature of the questions we ask, the manner in which we filter our information, and the methods we use to develop our answers.[6] Much as we may try to be "objective," subjectivity and relativity are inescapable in the social sciences.

The selection of evidence that has passed the tests of authenticity and reliability is a crucial issue. Research and writing is a continuous process of selection, first from your sources and then from your notes. Because the selection process is influenced by the researcher's subjective perspective, it calls for extreme care and integrity. Since subjective selection is such an integral feature of humanities and social science research, consensus is rare in the study of human affairs. You will discover that a range of equally valid opinions and theories exist on controversial issues — among authorities and even among your peers. Likewise, there is no final proof and no ultimate truth — most conclusions and interpretations in the humanities and social sciences are tentative at best.

Bias and subjectivity are not interchangeable terms. Subjectivity (or frame of reference) may be defined as the manner in which people perceive, understand, and interpret the world according to their personal code of values. Bias (or prejudice) is the conscious selection of evidence to support a preconceived position.[7] Subjectivity is unavoidable. Bias is unethical.

THE ROUGH DRAFT

If you arranged the sections of the Point-form Outline on separate pages, it is now easy to arrange them in the most appropriate order. Having worked extensively on the detailed outlines, you should have a clear idea of the relative importance of each section. Once you have rearranged the sections of your Point-form Outline, the shape of your paper will have emerged. With a detailed structure in place, it is a relatively easy task to start weaving the essay. * Having completed the outlines, you should not be afflicted by "writer's block" at this point: your course will be mapped clearly for you. Another advantage is that detailed outlines provide a formula for developing your paragraphs as demonstrated on page 44. All the work that went into preparing the outlines will now pay off. However, do not attempt to write your final copy straight from your Point-form Outline. Preparing a rough draft first will ensure a better essay.

One matter to consider (and discuss with your instructor) is whether you should address arguments and ideas that run counter to your thesis, or whether you should ignore opposing viewpoints. In shorter papers you will probably not have the space, but in longer research assignments, challenging counter arguments will lend an enhanced credibility to your thesis. Rebuttals should be inserted where they fit most naturally into the overall structure of the essay, and they must be included in planning the detailed outlines. There are three likely places in the essay where you can refute contradictory viewpoints:

- In the first paragraph of the body immediately after the thesis statement.

- In the body of the essay where you develop and substantiate your thesis.

- In footnotes or endnotes.

---

* There are a number of conventions of essay writing, such as quoting and documenting, that should be followed. These are discussed in sections V Quotations and VI Documentation. Consult these sections before proceeding with the rough draft since you will have to enter your citations in the draft. Because clarity of communication is so essential, you might wish to consult section IV on Style before writing the preliminary draft. Definitely consult it before writing the final draft.

How long should the essay be? This is one of the most common questions raised by students. In many cases the length of the paper will be determined by your instructor. If your instructor specifies a certain number of words, stay within 10 percent of the specified figure. If no word limit is set, the length will be established by the demands of the question and your response to it. Shorter rather than longer is a sound rule to follow. Remember that your words should be weighed, not counted.

If you are using a computer, you should take advantage of the fact that most word processors allow you to work on two documents at the same time, usually by splitting the screen into two "windows" as shown below. Bring up your outline in one window, and begin writing the essay in the other window. You can flip back and forth easily. You can also bring up the files that serve as your "electronic notes" in one window and transfer relevant information from that window into the window where you are writing the draft.

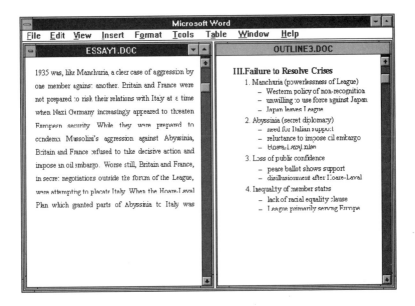

Screen Shot © 1983–1993 Microsoft Corporation, all rights reserved. Reprinted with permission from Microsoft Corporation.

Drafting the Introduction

The Introduction should prepare the reader by providing the background, such as setting the historical context, and by establishing the direction of the essay. Although usually short, introductions are important because they set the general tone of your work and because first impressions can influence the reader. Since essays and term papers are scholarly studies, it is inappropriate to inject humour and sensationalism into the Introduction to "grab" the reader's attention.

The coffee filter diagram offers an effective framework for an Introduction for a major term paper or extended essay.

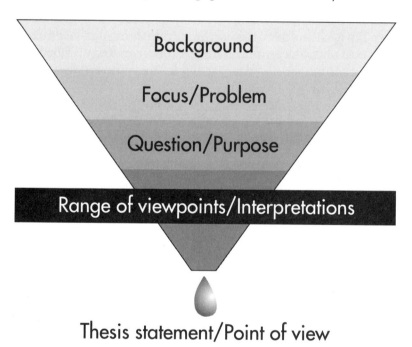

Background

Focus/Problem

Question/Purpose

Range of viewpoints/Interpretations

Thesis statement/Point of view

The coffee filter formula prepares the reader by first presenting the essential **background** information, which will be largely descriptive, narrative, or biographical. Next explain the **focus** (your problem or issue) of the essay and its importance as a field of study. Then you should indicate the **purpose** of your essay — to provide the reader with a signpost showing the direction of your project. Stating your research question is probably the clearest means of expressing the purpose of your essay. If you find it difficult to integrate a question smoothly into the text of the Introduction, try stating the objective of the assignment in a more traditional way such as, "The purpose of this paper is to explain why the League of Nations failed to maintain international stability in the 1930s."

The next step is to indicate the **range of viewpoints** and the nature of the intellectual debate surrounding your issue. You might even mention the articles and the specific works that feature these viewpoints and interpretations. If differing opinions do not exist, then simply omit this section in the Introduction. In such an instance, the coffee filter changes its shape to that of a funnel as shown below.[8]

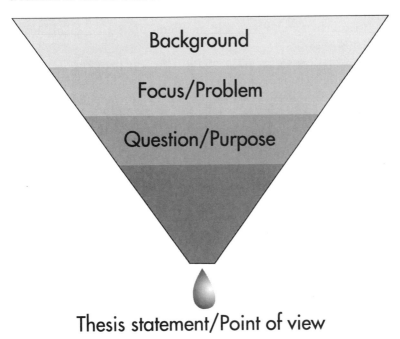

Background

Focus/Problem

Question/Purpose

Thesis statement/Point of view

Finally, state your argument or **thesis** (answer to your question) clearly. It is important to inform your readers of your position or point of view before you start developing the body of your essay. Academic papers are not detective thrillers aimed at keeping the reader in suspense until the final paragraph. Check with your instructor before using the first person in the thesis statement. Many instructors discourage the use of "I" in an essay.

Also ask your instructor whether the thesis statement should be a concise one or two sentence assertion or whether it should be an expanded explanation with details of the argument. Some instructors even recommend a description of the structure of the essay at the end of the Introduction. Definitions tend to interrupt the flow of the Introduction. It is advisable to place them in footnotes or endnotes.

Despite its brevity, the Introduction is an important and integral part of your essay. It will probably vary from about 10 percent to 20 percent of the overall length of the essay, but it must never overwhelm the body of your work. Check the details of the Introduction with your instructor, because some instructors may require only short Introductions of one or two paragraphs. No matter the length or the nature of the Introduction, remember to mention the three P's — **the problem, the purpose, and your point of view**.

On the opposite page, you will find the Introduction to the League of Nations essay. The coffee filter or funnel components, which are simply the subsections of the Skeleton Outline (page 33), provide the paragraph structure. The Introduction is shown here in final form after revising and editing.

The League of Nations was conceived during the carnage of the First World War. In an attempt to prevent the reoccurrence of an international tragedy of this scale, the peacemakers included the Covenant of the League in the peace treaties that concluded the war. The League had two main objectives: to promote peace by the collective collaboration of member states against an aggressor and to improve social and economic conditions worldwide.

The attempt to establish an international organization to maintain peace and balance power relationships among members was not new. The Congress of Vienna had been formed after the Napoleonic Wars and brought peace to Europe for many decades. Likewise, the United Nations, successor to the League of Nations, has had relative success in avoiding major conflagrations. Yet within two decades of the formation of the League, Europe embarked on a bloody war that eventually engulfed most of the world. The tragically short period of peace raises the question why the League of Nations failed to maintain international stability in the 1930s.

Writers have suggested many reasons. The founding charter, the Covenant, was not only flawed, but its inclusion in the peace treaties caused resentment among the defeated powers. The absence of the United States as a member and the lack of commitment by major powers such as Germany, the USSR, Italy, and Japan relegated the burden to Britain and France. The structure of the League discouraged collective and decisive action against aggressors. Factors outside its control, such as the Great Depression, affected the role of the League. Major crises such as the invasions of Manchuria and Abyssinia and the failure of the World Disarmament Conference finally doomed the League.

The failure of the League can be attributed to a combination of three factors. Flaws in the Covenant limited the League's power and affected enforcement of its decisions. Support for collective security among the major powers was half-hearted. Finally, the League's failure to resolve the Manchurian and Abyssinian crises meant that it was discredited at the very time it was most needed — to halt the rise of Nazism.

Drafting the Body

With a completed Point-form Outline it is a relatively easy task to weave the body of your essay in a rough draft. Your outlines, in addition to ensuring structure, also arrange your paragraphs. We have reproduced B. III Failure to Resolve Crises, from page 35, to illustrate how the subsections of the Skeleton Outline provide the paragraph structure, while the details of the Point-form Outline supply the supporting information for each paragraph. The transformation of B. III from outline to paragraphed copy is shown below.

B. III FAILURE TO RESOLVE CRISES	(introductory paragraph)
1. Manchuria (powerlessness of League) — Western policy of non-recognition — unwilling to use force against Japan — Japan leaves League	(paragraph)
2. Abyssinia (secret diplomacy) — need for Italian support — reluctance to impose oil embargo — Hoare–Laval plan	(paragraph)
3. Loss of public confidence — peace ballot shows support — disillusionment after Hoare–Laval	(paragraph)
4. Inequality of member states — lack of racial equality clause — League primarily serving Europe	(paragraph)
	(concluding paragraph)

The structural problems of the League of Nations and the duplicity of the major powers became apparent during both the Manchurian and Abyssinian crises. The League's failure to resolve these disputes in a manner consistent with its charter resulted in the loss of both public and political confidence in the organization, discrediting it at the time when it was most needed — the beginning of Hitler's expansion in Europe.

The Japanese invasion of Manchuria in September 1931 and the establishment the following year of the puppet state of Manchukuo presented the League with a conflict between two Pacific powers. One member, Japan, had violated the territorial rights of another, China. Instead of invoking corrective force, the Western powers that controlled the League and had commercial ties with Japan merely refused to recognize Manchukuo. In the words of F.P. Walters (1952), ". . . the aggression had taken place, vast territories had been taken from the victim, and yet all they had done was to refuse to recognize the new state" (499). The League was not prepared to take decisive action and provoke a crisis in a region where the commercial interests of its influential members might be at risk. Japan's reaction was to resign from the League, further weakening the organization.

Mussolini's invasion of Abyssinia in October 1935 was, like Manchuria, a clear case of aggression by one member against another. Britain and France were not prepared to risk their relations with Italy at a time when Nazi Germany increasingly appeared to threaten European security. While they were prepared to condemn Mussolini's aggression against Abyssinia, Britain and France refused to take decisive action and impose an oil embargo. Worse still, Britain and France, in secret negotiations outside the forum of the League, were attempting to placate Italy. When the Hoare–Laval Plan, which granted parts of Abyssinia to Italy, was exposed, it also revealed the duplicitous nature of Franco–British policy. The Abyssinian crisis was a decisive event in the decline of the League.

The League of Nations enjoyed widespread support as a mechanism for resolving the Abyssinian crisis. In Britain, a "peace ballot" had been held, indicating vast popular support for the League. The Hoare–Laval plan was viewed by the public as government betrayal and as a sign of incompatibility between the spirit of the League and the reality of European diplomacy. Disillusionment set in and British public support for the League was "cast adrift as the government attempted to cover the tracks of its duplicity and confusion, following the path of appeasement and gradual rearmament" (Egerton, 1983, 514).

The European treatment of both Manchuria and Abyssinia demonstrated the inequality of member states in the League. Inequality was actually built into the organization because the architects of the League refused to enshrine racial equality in the Covenant. The violation of the territorial integrity of **any** member state deserved condemnation and appropriate action. Before taking such action, however, European powers first appeared to assess the diplomatic, political, and commercial costs. The nations of Europe, especially those with colonial interests, seemed far better served by the League of Nations than those states on the periphery of power.

The failure of the League to resolve the conflicts in Manchuria and Abyssinia in a manner consistent with both the spirit and the content of the Covenant discredited the organization. That the failure of collective security coincided with the expansion of Hitler's Germany finally doomed the League. It was sadly ironic that in the latter part of the decade many European nations would suffer the same fate as Manchuria and Abyssinia.

You will notice from the example on the previous two pages that each major section of the body follows a miniature ABC structure. An introductory paragraph "introduces" the section, "body" paragraphs develop the main point (the League's failure to resolve major crises), and a concluding paragraph sums up the section.

A paragraph is a series of sentences addressing **one** major idea or step in the development of your argument. The ABC formula also operates at the individual paragraph level. A topic sentence (not necessarily the first sentence) clearly states the main idea, followed by sentences that provide supporting detail. A concluding sentence sums up the paragraph and clarifies its role in the development of your thesis. Give unity and cohesion to your paragraphs by eliminating information that is irrelevant to the main idea or focal point of each paragraph.

There should be a smooth flow to each paragraph as the sentences follow one another naturally and logically. The smooth flow should continue between the paragraphs. This can be achieved by the use of transitional words and phrases such as "furthermore," "consequently," and "on the other hand" or by inserting transitional paragraphs. Paragraphs can be linked by using either the first sentence or the concluding sentence of each paragraph to make the transition. There is no standard length for paragraphs. They can vary from several to ten or more sentences depending on their significance and function. For example, transitional paragraphs will usually be shorter than paragraphs developing a major point.

The method described is not a rigid prescription for paragraphing; if you see a good reason to deviate from the pattern arising from the outlines, by all means do so. But bear in mind that some organizing scheme is essential. Paragraphs are like links in a chain. With proper paragraphing there is no need for subheadings in an essay. Subheadings tend to fragment the unity of an essay. Paragraphs with a central focus, explicit topic sentences, and suitable transitional words provide the unity, flow, and signposts that prevent the reader from getting lost in a maze of words.

The body of the essay is the most important section and the longest. It is devoted entirely to the development and substantiation of your thesis. Give the body of your essay the focus and clarity of a laser beam by explicitly linking all the information and the ideas to your thesis. Irrelevant information and extraneous details will fragment the focus of the essay. Instructors and examiners look for incisive analysis and argument in an essay, not for chronological narrative, rambling description, or irrelevant biographical details.

Before you start composing the rough draft of the body of the essay, remember:

- Incorporate the ideas in your *I.Q. Journal.*

- Read the sections on Quotations and Documentation carefully.

- Consult your instructor about special requirements, such as countering opposing viewpoints.

- Read section IV on Style.

- Consider your audience. Ensure that your "message" is clear.

- You are not "proving" your thesis; you are "supporting" it.

- Do not "stack the deck." Maintain a balanced and open-minded approach in composing your argument.

- Paragraphs should reflect the structure of your argument.

- Your responsibility is to construct and advance a systematic, logical, and convincing thesis — one that is carefully structured, persuasively argued, substantiated with evidence, and clearly expressed.

Drafting the Conclusion

The final section comprises your conclusions which form the most convincing answer to the question. In this section, you weave the various threads of the thesis and sum up the major supporting points. It should not be a dull restating of the major sections but a subtle linking of the main arguments. Sometimes it can be effective to start the Conclusion with the question since this reminds the reader of the purpose of the essay. But try to be more original than starting with a worn phrase such as, "in conclusion."

Do not add new information to support your thesis in the Conclusion since this will confuse the reader. If the information is important, it should be included with the development of the thesis in the body, not added as an afterthought to the Conclusion. Also do not insert quotations into the Conclusion for dramatic effect. In addition to summing up the thesis, you might place your issue within a wider context or perhaps discuss aspects that need further investigation. You might also identify unresolved questions or show the broader significance of your work and suggest implications for further research.

The Conclusion is brief, usually one paragraph, but it is important because it is the last opportunity to impress the reader with the validity of your arguments. Remember that last impressions are usually lasting impressions. Below you will find the Conclusion of the League of Nations essay. It is shown in final form after revising and editing.

The League of Nations was a bold attempt to provide a mechanism for maintaining collective security following the devastation of the First World War. Unfortunately, the League was unable to fulfill its mandate due to the combination of serious flaws in the Covenant that severely limited the exercise of its authority and by the determination of a number of member states to pursue an independent diplomatic agenda. Global society needs a means of curbing the competing interests of major powers and protecting the needs of weaker states. The League, despite its failures, was a noble experiment and an important step toward the realization of a more secure international society.

REVISING AND EDITING

Once you have typed or written your draft you are ready to start revising and editing. The clarity of the argument you are presenting and developing is determined largely by the **structure** of your answer and the **style** of your expression. Revising involves reviewing the draft for **structure** and **organization**. Editing involves refining the **style** and **expression** of the revised draft. This is an important stage and **you must allow time in your schedule for revising and editing**.

Set the draft aside for a few days before starting to revise it. Getting a little "distance" can sharpen your eye considerably. If you based your rough draft on a Point-form Outline, you will reduce the amount of revising substantially. The extra work that went into the preparatory stages invariably pays off in the long run.

Your first task is to examine the order of the main sections of the body. Although you may have rearranged the structure at the Point-form Outline stage, the order might not work well when you write the rough draft. Whether you place your most important section first or last is a matter of personal preference. The question to ask yourself is whether there is a logical flow in the sequence of the sections.

Check the Introduction to make sure that both the purpose and your point of view are spelled out clearly. Does the Conclusion serve its purpose?

Once you are satisfied with the overall structure, look closely at the paragraphing. Circle the topic sentence in each paragraph to ensure that there is a central focal point. Is there sufficient supporting detail in each paragraph? Is there unity to each paragraph? Have you eliminated unnecessary words and phrases? Do the quotations fit? Do the paragraphs flow? Are all topic sentences linked to the thesis? These are the questions you should ask yourself as you revise your draft. But above all, ask yourself whether the essay develops a clear point of view.

The major changes are made at the revision stage. If you have many changes, it may be necessary to rewrite your draft. This is not wasted time because a further draft will improve the quality of the final copy. In the words of well-known author William Zinsser, "Writing is rewriting."[9] The next step is to read your draft aloud. You can read it to yourself or record it. You may read it to someone else or perhaps have that person read it while you listen. If it is difficult to read and sounds stilted, revise it until it flows smoothly and naturally.

Since editing is largely concerned with fine-tuning your language and expression, you should reread section IV on Style. It is a good practice to have a thesaurus, a dictionary, and a manual of style close at hand when you are editing your draft.

- Read through slowly, checking spelling and grammar carefully.
- Does your punctuation improve the flow of the essay?
- Have you chosen your words carefully?
- Can you vary the structure and length of your sentences?
- Check your draft for discriminatory language.
- Is the tone of your paper formal?
- Is your quoting, documenting, and listing of sources accurate?
- Is the title concise and clear?

Once you have completed the editing, read the essay aloud another time. An essay that "speaks well" is invariably an essay that reads well. James Michener twice read aloud all 1238 pages of the manuscript of *The Covenant* before he was satisfied with it. The extra time spent in revising and editing is well worth it. There is a close relationship between effort and quality, and a good piece of work will always reflect the care taken in its preparation.

The word processor is a valuable editing tool. It can speed up the revising and editing, and enhance the quality of your papers. The advantage of word processing is that once the essay has been composed and keyed in, revision can be done without rewriting or rekeying the draft. Careful structuring, outlining, and drafting is necessary before processing the essay on a computer. A word processor has more important uses than merely shifting paragraphs in a disorganized piece of writing.

It is not always easy to get a feel for the overall structure of an essay on a video monitor, nor is it easy to detect punctuation or spelling errors. Many students find it easier to revise and edit on a printed copy of the draft. And it means someone else can also read and check it. You can then make the changes on the screen and print another copy for further editing.

If you are revising and editing on the screen, you may wish to keep all your electronic drafts. In this case simply name each revision, such as "ESSAY1," "ESSAY2," and so on. This will allow you to return to earlier revisions for material that you deleted in later versions. After you have produced your final copy, you can erase the earlier revisions. It is important that you frequently save your draft on both the hard drive and on a floppy disk to avoid losing your essay if there is a power failure or your hard drive malfunctions. **Instructors no longer accept the excuse of a "computer crash."**

If your word processor has a spell check, thesaurus, or a grammar check program, take advantage of it before printing the final draft. But remember that you must edit your work carefully even after you have used the software program, because although spell checks are very advanced, they have no way of knowing that when you wrote "to" you meant to write "too" or "two."

THE FINAL COPY

Leave yourself enough time to set aside your edited draft for a few days before you prepare the final copy. Your essay or paper is the product of a lengthy and intensive process. Much of the process never appears in the final product, but it is nevertheless essential to the quality of the final product. Although your research methods, notes, and drafts are sometimes evaluated, frequently instructors will base their assessment solely on the essay that is submitted—the one-tenth of the iceberg above the water. Proofread the final copy meticulously and assemble it with care. The final packaging is important because the overall appearance of the essay can create a positive initial impact.

Preparing your final copy should be quick and painless if you have used a word processor for writing and editing. The appearance of your essay can be improved by computer technology. Software programs can ensure a clean, professional type and provide a variety of graphic illustrations. Most schools and universities have computer facilities that are accessible to students so there is no need to purchase expensive equipment. Although not all instructors require typed assignments, combining literary ability with typing and computing skills is an important asset today. But remember that it is substance that characterizes a good essay. Technological dazzle alone is insufficient.

The major features of the final copy are covered in the following pages and illustrated with examples from the League of Nations essay. You will have read the sections on Quotations and Documenting Sources before writing your first draft. Check these sections again carefully when preparing your final copy because they contain examples from the League of Nations essay illustrating the conventions of quoting, documenting, and listing sources. These conventions must be observed accurately in your essay.

Individual instructors sometimes have their own preferences with regard to format, so it is advisable to check manuscript requirements before starting the final copy. If your instructor has expressed no specific preference, format your essay in this manner:

- Use standard-sized white unlined paper.

- Type (or write) on one side of the page only.

- Double-space the text.

- Leave at least a 2.5-cm margin all the way around the page.

- Number pages consecutively in arabic numerals in the upper right corner.

- Avoid section headings, as they tend to disrupt the argument.

- Leave a triple or quadruple space between the Introduction and the Body, and between the Body and the Conclusion. These spaces indicate important divisions.

- A "ragged" right margin is recommended because the text is easier to read than is text with justified right margins, which can create uneven spacing.

- Do not staple the pages together if you are using endnotes because instructors often like to remove the endnotes and refer to them as they read the essay. Use a paperclip instead.

- Avoid the use of folders.

- Always keep a backup copy of your essay. Keep your notes and drafts as well: they are your best defence against a charge of plagiarism.

Title Page

The Title Page should be simple, clear, and neat. The following information is normally required on title pages for essays:

1. Title: clear and concise but not normally in question form. Use a subtitle only if it helps to clarify the title.

2. Student name.

3. Course or class.

4. Instructor.

5. School/University/College.

6. Date.

The League of Nations and
Collective Security:
Failure of a Dream

S.M. Conway
History 101

Professor Z. Arbenz
Norwood College
March 1994

Table of Contents

A Contents page provides the reader with an outline of the structure of your essay. The letters of the alphabet in our example below correspond to the numbering used throughout the research and drafting stages. Avoid using the term "Body" in your Contents. It was used in the research and in the outlines to assist you in understanding the structure of an essay. Instead of "Contents," you may use "Outline." Many instructors do not require a table of contents. There is no need to include page references unless you are writing a dissertation.

CONTENTS

A. INTRODUCTION
B.

   I   STRUCTURE OF THE LEAGUE
   II   MOTIVES OF MEMBER STATES
   III   FAILURE TO RESOLVE CRISES

C. CONCLUSION
D. APPENDIX
E. WORKS CONSULTED

Illustrations

Illustrations can be very effective in essays. There are two major types of illustrations: tables and figures. Tables contain columns of statistical data. Figures consist of photographs, maps, drawings, graphs, diagrams, charts, and pictures.

Tables and figures are usually placed at the appropriate spot in the text of the essay. If they are lengthy, they can be placed in the Appendix. Select illustrations carefully and do not overwhelm your essay with too many pictures, maps, and graphs. Ask yourself whether each table or figure actually illustrates a point in your essay.

Examples of various types of illustrations are shown on pages 105–109 in the Appendix.

Appendix

The Appendix is a useful place at the end of your essay for important information that is too extensive to be placed in the body. The material must be relevant to the thesis of your paper and must be cross-referenced in either a footnote or a parenthetical reference. Guard against the temptation to pack the Appendix with unnecessary material.

A history paper might include a speech or a chronology of events in the Appendix. Statistical tables might be placed in the appendices of geography and economics essays. The Appendix is placed before the Bibliography and Endnotes (if used), and each item is numbered and titled. See pages 91–119 of this manual for an example.

Both illustrations and material in the Appendix must be used judiciously and explicitly linked to your thesis. Never use them to pad your essay or dress it up.

STYLE

Style is the manner of your writing rather than the substance of your essay.[10] Every person's writing style is unique. Although your style reflects your personality, your style must still be governed by the conventions of language usage. You cannot adopt a style that departs drastically from orthodox sentence structure and commonly accepted forms of punctuation if you wish to communicate effectively. In other words, you are free to be yourself, but there are limits.

Many manuals have been published on English usage and writing style. This book does not claim to be a style manual. However, this section does offer some practical tips on how to become proficient at the craft of writing research papers.

Read

Read as many books and magazines as you can. If you find a particular piece of writing effective, try to determine why it was effective. If you encounter new words, as you undoubtedly will, add them to your vocabulary. Reading the editorials in reputable newspapers and magazines is good training for essay writing, since editorials are often mini-essays with arguments based on evidence.

Write

Like sports stars and chess players, good writers develop their craft through practice and application. Experiment with the different writing techniques you have identified through your reading. As with most skills, successful style is usually 10 percent inspiration and 90 percent perspiration.

Clarity

Clarity of expression is one of the key features of a successful style. Brevity, simplicity, and precision are the essential qualities of clear style. Eliminate the clutter of unnecessary words.[11] For instance, do not say, "At that point, Napoleon's empire was as big as it was going to get," when you can say "Napoleon's empire reached its zenith in 1809."

Vocabulary

Careful selection of words not only ensures clarity of meaning, it also enhances the sound and harmony of your writing. Always choose concrete words over vague terms and abstract generalizations. A reputable dictionary and a thesaurus will assist you in the judicious selection and use of words.

Fluency

Good writing has an even flow. Give your writing rhythm and harmony by your choice of words and your use of punctuation. For instance, you can use transitional words such as "nevertheless," "consequently," and "furthermore" to link the flow of ideas; and you can use pre-planned punctuation structures — such as a series of clauses linked by semi-colons — to present your ideas to their best advantage. Test your writing for eloquence by reading it aloud and then fine-tune it until it flows smoothly and naturally.

Tone

An essay should have a formal and scholarly tone. Contractions such as "can't" and "won't" may be part of everyday speech but they should not be used in formal writing. Likewise, slang, jargon, and trendy, overused expressions such as "prioritize" have no place in an essay.

Jargon

Every academic discipline has its own jargon and code words. Some of these words are necessary and useful since they can define a concept with great precision, but some of them are no more than big words designed to impress a reader. These words usually obscure the meaning of the essay. A good essay is not something written in a secret code that only the writer and the instructor can understand; a good essay should be accessible to any intelligent reader.

Discriminatory Language

Never use language that discriminates on the grounds of sex, race, or religion. Language that stereotypes people and groups is unacceptable in any type of writing. In particular, avoid using the masculine pronoun when referring to human groups that could legitimately be male or female, or comprised of both sexes. Guides are available to help you substitute words and expressions that are free of discrimination.

Grammar

Language usage is based on rules and conventions that serve to clarify comprehension. If you ignore rules and conventions, you will do only one thing: you will obscure the message of your essay.

Sentences

Vary the length of your sentences to change the pace of your writing. Shorter sentences can be used to give emphasis to a point. Make sure that every sentence really is a sentence, with a proper subject and a verb.

Tenses

Research papers are usually written in the past tense. But writing in the past tense does not mean that you should adopt a "passive" sentence structure. Use active verbs to give force to your writing. Do not say, "Napoleon was beaten at the battle of Waterloo by Wellington" when you can say, "Wellington defeated Napoleon at the battle of Waterloo."

Punctuation

Pay attention to punctuation. Good punctuation can improve the readability and clarity of your essay to a remarkable degree. Since an essay is a formal piece of writing, minimize the use of the dash, and avoid using the exclamation mark entirely.

Pronouns

Consensus on the use of pronouns in essay writing does not exist among instructors. Some accept the use of the first person "I," others decry its use. Some prefer "the author" or "the writer," while others regard these terms as pretentious. "We" or "one" find acceptance with some instructors, but not with others. However, there is near unanimity on avoiding the use of the second person pronoun "you" in formal academic writing.

Spelling

Careless spelling can mar an otherwise well-written essay. Use a dictionary or the spell check function on the computer to eliminate errors.

A pleasing style is not based solely on rigid and mechanically correct English. Attempt to breathe vitality, enthusiasm, and colour into your writing. Do not be discouraged if your first efforts do not create the effects you want: developing a good writing style requires dedication and application, effort and practice. But the payoff is worth it, for a pleasing style will not only enhance the clarity of your essay, it will also add a persuasive element to your arguments.

QUOTATIONS

In the humanities and the social sciences, the researcher relies on both primary sources and on previous scholarship in the form of secondary sources. An important decision facing students is when to use paraphrased ideas and information and when to quote directly from the source material. Quotations, from either primary or secondary sources, can be used effectively in the following situations:

- As evidence to illustrate and provide credibility for your arguments.

- As support to add authority to your point of view.

- To lend elegance and eloquence to your writing.

- To quote the author's central argument when challenging an opposing viewpoint.

- When the original words express the meaning better than is possible by paraphrasing.

A cardinal rule in writing essays and papers is: **Do not overquote.** Quotations must be used sparingly and judiciously. A paper strung together like a patchwork quilt of quotations is not an essay. Not only will the excessive use of quotations destroy the clarity of your arguments, but "to indulge yourself too often in the quoting of others' great thoughts is to run the risk of never learning to formulate your own."[12]

Quotations by themselves do not constitute indisputable evidence. It is the strength of your arguments that will convince the reader of the validity of your thesis. Therefore, quotations must be anchored firmly in the text of your essay and linked explicitly to the thesis. They should not be parachuted into the essay simply for dramatic effect and as space fillers. While excerpts from secondary sources may indicate the breadth and depth of your research, mere name-dropping of authorities for effect should be avoided.

Not only should you select your quotations carefully, but you should keep them short. Remember that clarity of argument is your key objective. Cluttering your essay with lengthy, irrelevant quotations does not enhance clarity. Does each quotation serve a purpose? If not, eliminate it.

When quoting other authors, it is essential to cite the sources of their ideas. There are procedures for acknowledging your sources, thereby ensuring that you are not guilty of plagiarism. These citation procedures have been omitted from the quotation examples that follow to avoid confusion. They are explained in detail in the next section on Documentation.

Short, single-sentence quotations should be incorporated within the text of the essay and placed in double quotation marks. The quoted material should be woven into your writing and merged as naturally as possible within the text.

Example:

Sociologist Nadine Brenton argues that "there is a direct correlation between low taxes and violent crime in society."

If a longer quotation is necessary and it consists of two or more sentences and four or more lines, it should be separated from the text. The quoted passage (also known as a block quotation) starts on a new line and is usually introduced with a colon. A block quotation is indented between 4 and 10 spaces from the left margin, depending on the preferences of your instructor or on the recommendation of a manual you may be using. Block quotations are usually single-spaced and quotation marks are omitted. Check spacing requirements with your instructor if you are uncertain.

squeeze from both sides

Example:

Alderson, who commanded the regiment for most of its tour of duty, wrote to Lessard:

> I have just come back from the station where I went to see your people off . . . and I should like to write and tell you how very sincerely sorry I am that they have left. We have soldiered together for seven months and during that time a firm bond developed.

If it is necessary to omit part of a quotation because of length or irrelevancy, use three spaced periods (. . .) as shown in the previous example. This is known as an ellipsis. However, you must not alter the meaning of the passage or make it incomprehensible through your own omission of words. You must also ensure that the modified quotation is grammatically correct.

If you have to insert words in a quotation to clarify its meaning, enclose them in square brackets.

Example:

"The role [of the Mounted Infantry] is to act as an advance guard."

If an error is present in the quoted material, use the Latin word *sic* (meaning "so" or "thus") to indicate it. Use square brackets and italicize or underline *sic*.

Example:

"The Police Chief denied that the prisonners [*sic*] had been refused water."

Single quotation marks are used where a quotation occurs within quoted material.

Example:

"Noble wrote in his diary that he had been subjected to 'cruel and unusual punishment' during his confinement."

Generally, punctuation marks such as commas and periods are placed within the quotation marks, while colons, semicolons, question marks, and exclamation marks go outside the quotation marks. However, any punctuation mark that is part of the quoted material is included within the quotation marks.

Do not burden the text with excessively long quotations over 7 or 10 lines long; they should be placed in the appendix and referred to in a note or a parenthetical reference.

It is essential that you quote the material, including the punctuation, accurately. Hence the importance of transcribing quotations carefully during your research. To alter the wording or meaning of a quotation or to use a quotation out of context is unethical.

Further information on the conventions of quoting may be obtained from one of the recommended manuals or from your instructor. Above all, be consistent in the method you use for quoting.

DOCUMENTATION

INTRODUCTION

I t is essential that you identify the sources you have used to develop and substantiate your arguments. **Both direct quotations and paraphrased ideas must be acknowledged.** Failure to document your sources constitutes plagiarism: a serious academic offence. Just as ignorance of the law is no excuse, there is no excuse for "accidental" plagiarism. However, factual information that is common knowledge need not be documented. For instance, you do not have to document a source stating that the League of Nations was founded in 1919.

Frequently, determining what is common knowledge is not easy, but your judgement will improve with practice. It is especially important to document the evidence when you are developing a controversial point. **Document when in doubt is a safe rule to follow,**[13] but do not overdo the use of citations. It is a mistake to attempt to impress the reader with reams of footnotes or parenthetical citations. Common sense as well as ethics should govern your use of citations.[14]

Citing the authorities for information used in your paper gives credit to other writers for their ideas. Basing your research on sound scholarship also enhances its credibility. Providing the sources enables the information to be checked for accuracy and guides the reader to additional sources of information on the topic.

Four major documentation or citation styles are used for writing assignments in the social sciences, the humanities, and the natural and physical sciences. Since students are often required to take courses in a broad range of disciplines, you should be conversant with these documentation systems. You will notice that two are parenthetical in-text systems, and two are numbered systems. Furthermore, two tend to be popular in the humanities, while the other two are used more commonly in the sciences.

- **Author/Page:** The source is indicated by providing the author's last name and the page reference in a parenthetical citation in the text of the essay. The reader can then refer to a list of sources at the end of the essay to obtain complete bibliographic details. This method is described in the *MLA Handbook for Writers of Research Papers* published by The Modern Language Association of America. The MLA procedures are used widely in language and literature.

- **Author/Date:** The source is indicated by providing the author's last name and the year of publication of the work in a parenthetical citation in the text of the essay. A page reference may sometimes be included. The reader can then refer to a list of sources at the end of the essay to obtain complete bibliographic details. This method is described in the *Publication Manual* of the American Psychological Association (APA), *The Chicago Manual of Style*, and in *Scientific Style and Format: The CBE Manual for Authors, Editors, and Publishers*. The Author/Date system is used widely in the social sciences, business, and the natural sciences.

- **Footnotes/Endnotes:** The source is indicated by using a superscript number in the text, which corresponds to an entry in a footnote or endnote containing complete bibliographic details. This method is described in *The Chicago Manual of Style*, Kate Turabian's *A Manual for Writers of Term Papers, Theses, and Dissertations*, and the *MLA Handbook for Writers of Research Papers*. Documentary notes are used widely in humanities subjects such as history, philosophy, religion, classics, and the arts.

- **Number Reference:** The source is indicated by using a number in brackets or parentheses in the text. A corresponding number in the list of sources at the end of the essay provides complete bibliographic details. This method is described in *Scientific Style and Format*, *A Manual for Authors of Mathematical Papers*, and in the *Style Guide* of the American Chemical Society. The numbered reference method is used mainly in the physical, applied, and medical sciences.

Two documentation systems widely used in the humanities and social sciences are described in this manual: the numbered footnote/endnote system and the parenthetical author/date system. The basic elements of each are explained under identical headings: Documenting Sources, Explanatory Notes, and Listing Sources. Examples of documenting and listing the more common types of sources are also provided. Because the description of each system can be read independently, there is some unavoidable repetition.

In this manual, the author/date system has been used in the sample essay; the manual itself uses numbered endnotes. Always check with your instructor to determine the preferred method of documentation for each essay. Remember, whichever method you choose, make sure that you follow the method throughout your essay to ensure consistency, simplicity, and clarity.

FOOTNOTES/ENDNOTES

Documenting Sources

Sources can be acknowledged and identified by a numbered note system. An arabic numeral is placed above the line at the end of the sentence or quotation, and these citation references are numbered consecutively throughout the paper. The superscript numbers follow all punctuation marks except the dash. Each of these numbers corresponds to an entry in either a footnote at the bottom of the page or to an endnote near the end of the essay.

Traditionally, footnotes have been used as documentary notes. Information in a footnote is more accessible than in an endnote, and this is especially true when reading dissertations in microform. Word processing programs make it relatively easy to use the footnote format. Footnotes are separated from the text by a solid line 20 spaces in length. Leave a blank line and indent the same number of spaces as your regular paragraph indentions. If you are using block paragraphs, then use six spaces for indenting your footnotes. Type the superscript number followed by the citation details without an intervening space. Single-space any notes that continue on a second line, but leave a double space between individual citation notes. When a work is mentioned in a note for the first time, the complete entry is given. Subsequent references use a shortened form as explained on page 73. If there is no place of publication given, use n.p.; for no publisher use n.p.; and if both are missing, it is permissible to use just n.p. If no date is provided, insert n.d.

Another method is to place all citations on a separate page just before the Bibliography. Title the page "Notes" or "Endnotes" and enter the details as explained above for footnotes. You can use either superscript numbers (as explained above) or numbers typed on the line. In the latter case only, the number is followed by a period and two spaces before the citation details are entered. See page 120 of this manual for an example of endnotes.

Examples of the more common forms of citation notes are shown on the next page. These examples are based on the procedures described in *A Manual for Writers* by Kate Turabian and in *The Chicago Manual of Style*.

Book

ONE AUTHOR

[1]James Barros, *Office Without Power* (Oxford: Clarendon Press, 1979), 91.

TWO AUTHORS

[2]V.A. Howard and J.H. Barton, *Thinking on Paper* (New York: William Morrow, 1986), 6.

MORE THAN THREE AUTHORS/EDITORS

[3]Joshua Brown et al., *History from South Africa: Alternative Visions and Practices* (Philadelphia: Temple University Press, 1991), 38.

EDITOR/COMPILER/TRANSLATOR

[4]John Tarrant, ed., *Farming and Food* (New York: Oxford University Press, 1991), 75.

NO AUTHOR

[5]*Beowulf*, trans. David Wright (Harmondsworth, England: Penguin Books, 1960), 45.

(Do not use *Anonymous* or *Anon.*)

CORPORATE AUTHOR

[6]American Psychological Association, *Publication Manual*, 4th ed. (Washington, D.C.: American Psychological Association, 1994), 102.

MULTIVOLUME WORK

[7]Will and Ariel Durant, *The Story of Civilization*, vol. 10, *Rousseau and Revolution* (New York: Simon and Schuster, 1965), 56.

ESSAY IN AN EDITED WORK

[8]Christopher Wrigley, "Changes in East African Society," in *A History of East Africa*, ed. D.A. Low and Alison Smith (Oxford: Oxford University Press, 1976), 3: 508.

LATER EDITION

[9]Mary-Claire van Leunen, *A Handbook for Scholars*, rev. ed. (New York: Oxford University Press, 1992), 49.

PAMPHLET

[10]G.O. Rothney, *Newfoundland: A History*, Historical Booklet, no. 10 (Ottawa: Canadian Historical Association, 1964), 5.

Encyclopedia

SIGNED ARTICLE
[11]*Encyclopedia of American Foreign Policy*, 1978 ed., s.v. "Isolationism," by Manfred Jones.

UNSIGNED ARTICLE
[12]*Canadian Encyclopedia*, 1988 ed., s.v. "Callwood, June."
(s.v. stands for *sub verso*, meaning "under the word.")

Newspaper

SIGNED ARTICLE
[13]Dale Harris, "The Real Thing,"*Wall Street Journal*, 17 June 1994, sec. A, p. 12.

UNSIGNED ARTICLE
[14]"Troubled by Rumours,"*Christian Science Monitor*, 10 June 1994, 17.

EDITORIAL
[15]"A Sobering Reminder," editorial, *Times of India*, 1 June 1994, 10.

LETTER TO THE EDITOR
[16]Simon Beare, letter, *Times* (London), 13 June 1994, 21.

Magazine

SIGNED ARTICLE
[17]David Osborne, "The Origins of Petroleum," *Atlantic*, February 1986, 50.

UNSIGNED ARTICLE
[18]"Quark Hunters," *Time*, 29 October 1990, 36.

Journal

CONTINUOUS PAGINATION
[19]I.L. Claude, "Casual Commitment to International Relations," *Political Science Quarterly* 96 (1981): 370.

SEPARATE PAGINATION
[20]Nancy C. Roberts, "Public Entrepreneurship and Innovation," *Policy Studies Review* 11 (spring 1992): 60.

Review

BOOK

[21]R. Towers, review of *Friend of My Youth*, by Alice Munro, *New York Review of Books*, 17 May 1990, 39.

FILM

[22]David Ansen, "How the West was Lost," review of *Dances with Wolves* (TIG/Orion movie), *Newsweek*, 19 November 1990, 67.

Interview

PERSONAL

[23]Edwin McCormick, interview by author, tape recording, Toronto, Ontario, 10 January 1980.

PUBLISHED

[24]Nadine Gordimer, "The Power of a Well-Told Tale," interview by P. Gray and B. Nelan, *Time*, 14 October 1991, 92.

RADIO/TELEVISION

[25]Nadine Gordimer, interview by Eleanor Wachtel, *Writers and Company*, CBC Stereo, 26 May 1991.

Conference Paper

[26]Richard W. Cottam, "Modern Diplomacy and Intervention" (paper presented at the 62nd annual meeting of the American Political Science Association, New York, 8–10 September 1966), 17–18.

Speech/Lecture

[27]M. Scott Peck, "A New Psychology of Love, Traditional Values, and Spiritual Growth," Lecture, The Centre of New Fire, Ottawa, 22 September 1990.

Dissertation

UNPUBLISHED

[28]Kimberly J. Thompson, "Continuity and Change: Women's Social Participation" (master's thesis, Cornell University, 1992), 67.

ABSTRACT

[29]Keith L. Shimko, "Images and Policy Debates" (Ph. D. diss. Indiana University, 1990), abstract in *Dissertation Abstracts International* 51A (1990): 1766 A.

Film

[30]*Dances with Wolves*, directed by Kevin Costner, TIG/Orion, Los Angeles, 1990.

Videocassette

[31]*Hamlet*, 225 min, BBC, London, 1987, videocassette.

Radio/Television Programs

[32]"Apartheid," produced by John Blake, *Frontline*, Public Broadcasting System, 10 May 1986.

Work of Art

[33]Pablo Picasso, *Still Life with Chair-Caning*, oil on canvas, 1912, Musée Picasso, Paris.

Map

[34]*Physical United States*, map (Washington, D.C.: National Geographic Society, 1987).

Public Document

[35]U.S. Department of State, *The Berlin Crisis: A Report on the Moscow Discussions, 1948* (Washington, D.C.: Government Printing Office, 1948), 39–40.

Manuscript

[36]Hare to father, letter, 16 April 1900, W.A. Hare Papers, National Archives, Ottawa.

Computer

PROGRAM

[37]Microsoft Multimedia Beethoven: The Ninth Symphony (1992), Microsoft Corporation, Redmond, Washington.

ELECTRONIC DOCUMENT

[38]R. Davis, a review of *A Question of Leadership*, by Michael Gordon, *Australian Electronic Journal of History* 1, no. 2 (June 1993): sec. 2; available from gopher to gopher.CIC.net, Electronic Serials Section; INTERNET.

Indirect Sources

[39]L. Curtis, *With Milner in South Africa* (Oxford: Oxford University Press, 1951), 87, quoted in Thomas Pakenham, *The Boer War* (London: Weidenfeld and Nicholson, 1979), 101.

All titles have been italicized in these examples. If you are using a word processor, titles may be boldfaced or italicized. In handwritten or typed essays, titles italicized in this guide would be underlined.

There is no need to give the complete entry for a subsequent reference to a source. If you have to refer to a work already cited in full, use an abbreviated format containing the author's surname and the page reference.

Example:

[6]Turabian, 168.

If more than one of Turabian's books has been used, you would have to include a shortened version of the title to identify it.

Example:

[6]Turabian, *Student's Guide,* 168.

If it is necessary to refer immediately to the same source, you may choose to use "ibid.," which is the abbreviated form of the Latin word "ibidem" meaning "in the same place." For example, an immediate reference to the same page of Turabian's book would be cited:

[7]Ibid.

If another citation to the same book by Turabian follows immediately, it would be entered in this way:

[8]Ibid., 170.

It is not essential, however, to use ibid. Instead, simply repeat the author's name and give the new page number. Some instructors do not like the use of ibid., and other Latin abbreviations such as "op. cit." are becoming obsolete.

Explanatory Notes

There is another type of note that has a very different function than the documentary or citation note. The explanatory note, sometimes called a supplementary, substantive, content, or discursive note, is used for additional information. This information, while relevant to the essay, could detract from the development of your argument if inserted directly in the text. For example, it may be necessary to provide additional biographical information on a person or give foreign currency equivalents. Translations, definitions, and acknowledgements may also be placed in explanatory notes. Cross-references to other parts of the paper or to material in the appendix can also be made in this type of note.

It is more convenient for the reader to refer to explanatory information at the bottom of the page than to have to turn to the end of the essay. If you are using endnotes to document your sources, it is easy to distinguish the explanatory notes by assigning asterisks (*) or other symbols (†) in the text to refer to the information in a footnote. For an example of an explanatory footnote, see page 16 of this guide. If you are using documentary footnotes rather than endnotes, then use one set of superscript numerals for both your documentary notes and your explanatory notes.

You must resist the temptation to place too much information in explanatory footnotes because this may distract the reader from the development of your argument in the text of the essay. If information is relevant and necessary but extensive, place it in the appendix. Then use an asterisk (or numeral) in the text to direct the reader to the footnote, which will refer to the material in the appendix. Alternatively, you may use a parenthetical reference in the text to refer the reader directly to the appendix.

Whatever method or combination of methods you use for explanatory material, it is important that you strive for **consistency, simplicity, and clarity.**

Listing Sources

As a general rule, it is recommended that you list **all** the information sources that proved **useful** in preparing the essay. Traditionally, this list has been called a Bibliography, and the term is still used widely. However, some instructors object to the use of the term for two reasons. First, the word bibliography literally means a list of books, and sources today range from books to interviews to databases. Secondly, bibliography implies a comprehensive and inclusive list of sources on a topic, and your sources are unlikely to represent an exhaustive list. Consider using alternative designations such as the following: *Works Consulted, Sources, Select Bibliography*.

Your sources should be listed in alphabetical order by author on a separate page at the end of the essay. **Do not number your sources**. A single list of sources should be adequate for most high-school and undergraduate essays. For longer research papers and dissertations you may be required to classify your sources into primary and secondary material or published and unpublished information. Note that the classified structure of the Working Bibliography recommended earlier in this guide suggested that sources be grouped under headings such as "Books," "Articles," and "Audio-Visual." This was to encourage a diversity of sources. The final list of sources should not be classified in this way. If an annotated bibliography is required you will have to make critical comments on the value of each source. See page 88 for an example.

The format for listing your sources is similar to the procedure for documenting your sources except for minor differences. One variation is the order of the names, and another is the indention of the entries. Each entry starts at the left margin with the author's surname listed first. If the entry extends beyond one line, the second and subsequent lines (which are usually single-spaced) are indented five spaces. Leave a double space between individual entries. If there is no place of publication given, use N.p.; for no publisher use n.p.; and if both are missing, it is permissible to use just N.p. If no date is provided, insert n.d.

Shown overleaf are examples of the more common types of sources. They are based on procedures described in *The Chicago Manual of Style* and Kate Turabian's *A Manual for Writers*. Students are advised to consult the manuals for further details and more specialized forms.

Book

ONE AUTHOR
Barros, James. *Office Without Power*. Oxford: Clarendon Press, 1979.

TWO AUTHORS
Howard, V.A. and J.H. Barton. *Thinking on Paper*. New York: William Morrow, 1986.

MORE THAN THREE AUTHORS/EDITORS
Brown, Joshua et al. *History from South Africa: Alternative Visions and Practices*. Philadelphia: Temple University Press, 1991.

EDITOR/COMPILER/TRANSLATOR
Tarrant, John, ed. *Farming and Food*. New York: Oxford University Press, 1991.

NO AUTHOR
Beowulf. Translated by David Wright. Harmondsworth, England: Penguin Books, 1960.
(Do not use *Anonymous* or *Anon.*)

CORPORATE AUTHOR
American Psychological Association. *Publication Manual*. 4th ed. Washington, D.C.: American Psychological Association, 1994.

MULTIVOLUME WORK
Durant, Will and Ariel. *The Story of Civilization*. Vol. 10, *Rousseau and Revolution*. New York: Simon and Schuster, 1965.

ESSAY IN AN EDITED WORK
Wrigley, Christopher. "Changes in East African Society." Vol. 3. In *A History of East Africa*, edited by D.A. Low and Alison Smith. Oxford: Oxford University Press, 1976.

LATER EDITION
van Leunen, Mary-Claire. *A Handbook for Scholars*. Rev. ed. New York: Oxford University Press, 1992.

PAMPHLET
Rothney, G.O. *Newfoundland: A History*. Historical Booklet, no. 10. Ottawa: Canadian Historical Association, 1964.

Encyclopedia

SIGNED ARTICLE
Encyclopedia of American Foreign Policy. 1978 ed. S.v. "Isolationism," by Manfred Jones.

UNSIGNED ARTICLE
Canadian Encyclopedia. 1988 ed. S.v. "Callwood, June."
(S.v. stands for *sub verso*, meaning "under the word.")

Newspaper

SIGNED ARTICLE

Harris, Dale. "The Real Thing." *Wall Street Journal*, 17 June 1994, sec. A, p. 12.

UNSIGNED ARTICLE

"Troubled by Rumours." *Christian Science Monitor*, 10 June 1994, 17.

EDITORIAL

"A Sobering Reminder." Editorial. *Times of India*, 1 June 1994, 10.

LETTER TO THE EDITOR

Beare, Simon. Letter. *Times* (London), 13 June 1994, 21.

Magazine

SIGNED ARTICLE

Osborne, David. "The Origins of Petroleum." *Atlantic*, February 1986, 39–54.

UNSIGNED ARTICLE

"Quark Hunters." *Time*, 29 October 1990, 36.

Journal

CONTINUOUS PAGINATION

Claude, I.L. "Casual Commitment to International Relations." *Political Science Quarterly* 96 (1981): 367–79.

SEPARATE PAGINATION

Roberts, Nancy C. "Public Entrepreneurship and Innovation." *Policy Studies Review* 11 (spring 1992): 55–74.

Review

BOOK

Towers, R. Review of *Friend of My Youth*, by Alice Munro. *New York Review of Books*, 17 May 1990, 38–39.

FILM

Ansen, David. "How the West was Lost." Review of *Dances with Wolves* (TIG/Orion movie). *Newsweek*, 19 November 1990, 67–68.

Interview

PERSONAL

McCormick, Edwin. Interview by author. Tape recording. Toronto, Ontario, 10 January 1980.

PUBLISHED

Gordimer, Nadine. "The Power of a Well-Told Tale." Interview by P. Gray and B. Nelan. *Time.* 14 October 1991, 92–93.

RADIO/TELEVISION

Gordimer, Nadine. Interview by Eleanor Wachtel. *Writers and Company.* CBC Stereo, 26 May 1991.

Conference Paper

Cottam, Richard W. "Modern Diplomacy and Intervention." Paper presented at the 62nd annual meeting of the American Political Science Association, New York, 8–10 September 1966.

Speech/Lecture

Peck, M. Scott. "A New Psychology of Love, Traditional Values, and Spiritual Growth." Lecture. The Centre of New Fire. Ottawa, 22 September 1990.

Dissertation

UNPUBLISHED

Thompson, Kimberly J. "Continuity and Change: Women's Social Participation." Master's thesis, Cornell University, 1992.

ABSTRACT

Shimko, Keith L. "Images and Policy Debates." Ph. D. diss., Indiana University, 1990. Abstract in *Dissertation Abstracts International* 51A (1990): 1766 A.

Film

Dances with Wolves. Directed by Kevin Costner. TIG/Orion, Los Angeles, 1990.

Videocassette

Hamlet. 225 min. BBC, London, 1987. Videocassette.

Radio/Television Programs

"Apartheid." Produced by John Blake. *Frontline.* Public Broadcasting System, 10 May 1986.

Work of Art

Picasso, Pablo. *Still Life with Chair-Caning*. Oil on canvas. 1912. Musée Picasso, Paris.

Map

Physical United States. Map. Washington, D.C.: National Geographic Society, 1987.

Public Document

U.S. Department of State. *The Berlin Crisis: A Report on the Moscow Discussions, 1948*. Washington, D.C.: Government Printing Office, 1948.

Manuscript

Hare, W.A. Papers. National Archives, Ottawa.

Computer

PROGRAM

Microsoft Multimedia Beethoven: The Ninth Symphony (1992). Microsoft Corporation, Redmond, Washington.

ELECTRONIC DOCUMENT

Davis, R. Review of *A Question of Leadership*, by Michael Gordon. *Australian Electronic Journal of History* 1, no. 2 (June 1993): sec. 2. Available from gopher to gopher.CIC.net, Electronic Serials Section; INTERNET.

Indirect Sources

Curtis, L. *With Milner in South Africa*, 87. Oxford: Oxford University Press, 1951. Quoted in Thomas Pakenham, *The Boer War* (London: Weidenfeld and Nicholson, 1979), 101.

All titles have been italicized in these examples. If you are using a word processor, titles may be boldfaced or italicized. In handwritten or typed essays, titles italicized in this guide would be underlined.

When listing two or more sources by the same author, enter the name for the first entry only. For the next entry (and successive entries) type a 3-em dash in place of the author's name. See the *Works Consulted* on page 121 for an example.

AUTHOR/DATE

Documenting Sources

Another method of acknowledging and identifying your sources is to provide the author's last name and the year of publication of the work in a parenthetical citation in the text. The reader can then refer to the list of sources at the end of the essay to obtain the bibliographic details.

Example:

The lack of any binding commitment on the part of League members was a major factor in its downfall (Northedge, 1986).

In the list of works at the end of the essay, the reference would be entered as follows:

Northedge, F.S. (1986). *The League of Nations: Its life and times, 1920–1946.* Leicester: Leicester University Press.

The in-text procedure enables the reader to determine the source quickly, but frequent parenthetical citations tend to disrupt the reader's flow of thought. Include just the essential citations. Improve readability by placing the citation at the end of a sentence or where a pause occurs, and include the author's name if possible in the sentence.

Example:

Nadine Brenton (1987) argues that "there is a direct correlation between low taxes and violent crime in society" (33).

Page numbers are necessary only if you use a direct quotation (as shown above) or if you refer to a specific section of the work. Page references may also be indicated as follows: (p. 33).

Some of the more common forms of parenthetical citations using the author/date system are shown on the following page. These examples are based largely on the procedures in the latest edition of the *Publication Manual* of the American Psychological Association (APA). Only the parenthetical citation is given here; the corresponding entry in the list of sources (References or Works Consulted) is shown separately on pages 84–87.

Citing a work by two authors:

Strunk and White (1979) recommend avoiding the use of qualifiers.

Citing a work by three to five authors:

Jackson, North, Hill, and Cruz (1990) discovered that . . . (first citation)

Jackson et al. (1990) discovered that . . . (subsequent citations)

Citing a work by six or more authors:

Hazen et al. (1993) describe how . . .

Citing a work by a corporate author:

The Committee on Famine Relief (1987) reports that agricultural practices have exacerbated the plight of refugees.

Citing a work with no author:

The Chicago Manual of Style (1993) offers an alternative documentation system.

Citing multiple works within the same parentheses:

American volunteers participated in the Boer War for different reasons (Strong, 1963; Williams, 1971).

Citing a multivolume work with a page reference:

Strindberg's complex dramatic structure is perfectly expressive of another key expressionistic idea: the illusory quality of time and space (Gassner, 1980, 2:780).

Citing a work with no date of publication:

In an interesting account published during the Depression (Preston, n.d.) . . . .

Citing indirect sources:

Curtis' explanation (cited in Pakenham, 1979) differs from . . . .

Explanatory Notes

Sometimes it is necessary to include information which, while relevant to the essay, could detract from the development of your argument if inserted directly into the text. This information can be isolated in a separate note called a content or supplementary note. For example, it may be necessary to explain foreign currency equivalents or provide additional biographical information on a person. Translations, definitions, and acknowledgements may also be placed in explanatory notes. Likewise, references to other sources may be inserted in a separate note.

Number your explanatory notes consecutively throughout the essay using superscript arabic numerals at the appropriate places in the text. You may enter your notes as footnotes at the bottom of the pages or place them on a separate page near the end of the essay. It is more convenient for the reader to refer to explanatory information at the bottom of the page than to have to turn to the end of the essay. This is especially true when reading dissertations in microform.

Footnotes are separated from the text by a solid line 20 spaces in length. Leave a blank line and indent five spaces. Then type the superscript number followed by the note. If the note continues beyond one line, start subsequent lines at the left margin and single-space. When another note follows on the same page, leave a double space between individual notes.

Another method is to place all your explanatory notes on a separate page at the end of the essay just before the list of sources. Title the page "Notes" and enter the details as explained above for footnotes.

You must resist the temptation to place too much information in explanatory notes because frequent reference, either to footnotes or to the back of the essay, will distract the reader from the development of the argument in the text. If information is relevant and essential, but extensive, place it in the appendix. Then use a parenthetical reference in the text to refer the reader to the appendix.

Listing Sources

Brief, in-text parenthetical citations have to be linked to a list of sources at the end of the essay. This list must contain all the important details of each source used in your essay. Some instructors may only require details of the **sources cited in the essay**. A list of cited sources is titled *References*, although alternative terms such as *Sources Cited, Literature Cited,* or *Works Cited* are usually acceptable. If, however, you included sources that proved useful in the preparation of your essay but were not all necessarily cited, you may use one of the following headings: *Works Consulted, Sources, Select Bibliography*.

Your sources should be listed in alphabetical order by author on a separate page at the end of the essay. **Do not number your sources.** Use a single list of sources for high-school and under-graduate essays. For longer research papers and dissertations you may be required to classify your sources into primary and secondary material or published and unpublished information. Note that the classified structure of the Working Bibliography recommended earlier in this guide suggested that sources be grouped under headings such as "Books," "Articles," and "Au-dio-Visual." This was to encourage a diversity of sources. The final list of sources should not be classified in this manner. If an annotated bibliography is required, you will have to make critical comments on the value of each source. See page 88 for an example.

Each entry starts at the left margin with the author's sur-name listed first, followed by the initials or first name. Next the publication date of the work is placed in parentheses. The title of the work follows the publication date. In the author/date system it is customary to capitalize only the first word of the title and of the subtitle and any proper nouns. Some instructors may prefer the traditional method of capitalization. Publication details complete the entry. If an entry extends beyond one line, the second and subsequent lines are indented three spaces. Entries may be single- or double-spaced, but double spacing is required between individual references.

Shown on the following pages are examples of the more common types of sources. They are based largely on the proce-dures described in the APA *Publication Manual*. Students are advised to consult the manual for further details and more specialized forms. APA style is only one of a number of author/date systems. Therefore it is important to clarify citation and reference procedures with your instructor before starting your essay.

Book

ONE AUTHOR
Barros, James. (1979). *Office without power*. Oxford: Clarendon Press.

TWO AUTHORS
Howard, V.A. and Barton, J.H. (1986). *Thinking on paper*. New York: William Morrow.

MORE THAN THREE AUTHORS / EDITORS
Brown, J., Manning, P., Shapiro, K., and Wiener, J. (1991). *History from South Africa: Alternative visions and practices*. Philadelphia: Temple University Press.

EDITOR / COMPILER / TRANSLATOR
Tarrant, John. (Ed.). (1991). *Farming and food*. New York: Oxford University Press.

NO AUTHOR
It happened in B.C. (1970). Vancouver, BC: Centennial '71 Committee. (Do not use *Anonymous* or *Anon.*)

CORPORATE AUTHOR
American Psychological Association. (1994). *Publication manual* (4th ed.). Washington, DC: Author.

MULTIVOLUME WORK
Durant, Will and Ariel. (1960–1965). *The story of civilization: Vol. 10. Rousseau and revolution*. New York: Simon and Schuster.

ESSAY IN AN EDITED WORK
Wrigley, Christopher. (1976). Changes in East African society. In D.A. Low and A. Smith (Eds.), *A history of East Africa* (Vol. 3). Oxford: Oxford University Press.

LATER EDITION
van Leunen, Mary-Claire. (1992). *A handbook for scholars* (Rev. ed.). New York: Oxford University Press.

PAMPHLET
Rothney, G.O. (1964). *Newfoundland: A history* (Historical Booklet, No. 10). Ottawa: Canadian Historical Association.

Encyclopedia
SIGNED ARTICLE
Jones, Manfred. (1978). Isolationism. In *The encyclopedia of American foreign policy* (2: 496–506). New York: Charles Scribner.

UNSIGNED ARTICLE
Callwood, June. (1988). In *The Canadian encyclopedia* (1: 318–319). Edmonton, Alberta: Hurtig Publishers.

Newspaper
SIGNED ARTICLE
Harris, Dale. (1994, June 17). The real thing. *The Wall Street Journal*, sec. A, p. 12.

UNSIGNED ARTICLE
Troubled by rumours. (1994, June 10). *The Christian Science Monitor*, 17.

EDITORIAL
A sobering reminder. (1994, June 1). [Editorial]. *The Times of India*, 10.

LETTER TO THE EDITOR
Beare, Simon. (1994, June 13). Tinned memories [Letter to the editor]. *The Times* (London), 21.

Magazine
SIGNED ARTICLE
Osborne, David. (1986, February). The origins of petroleum. *Atlantic*, 39–54.

UNSIGNED ARTICLE
Quark hunters. (1990, October 29). *Time*, 36.

Journal
CONTINUOUS PAGINATION
Claude, I.L. (1981). Casual commitment to international relations. *Political Science Quarterly*, 96, 367–379.

SEPARATE PAGINATION
Roberts, Nancy C. (1992). Public entrepreneurship and innovation. *Policy Studies Review*, 11 (1), 55–74.

Review
BOOK
Towers, R. (1990, May 17). [Review of the book *Friend of my youth*]. *New York Review of Books*, 38–39.

FILM

Ansen, David. (1990, November 19). How the west was lost [Review of the film *Dances with wolves*]. *Newsweek*, 67–68.

Interview

PERSONAL

McCormick, Edwin. (1980, January 10). [Interview by author]. Toronto, Ontario.

PUBLISHED

Gordimer, Nadine. (1991, October 14). The power of a well-told tale. [Interview by P. Gray and B. Nelan]. *Time*, 92–93.

RADIO/TELEVISION

Gordimer, Nadine. (1991, May 26). [Interview by Eleanor Wachtel]. *Writers and company*, CBC Stereo.

Conference Paper

Cottam, Richard W. (1966, September 9). *Modern diplomacy and intervention.* Paper presented at the 62nd annual meeting of the American Political Science Association, New York.

Speech/Lecture

Peck, M. Scott. (1990, September 22). *A new psychology of love, traditional values, and spiritual growth.* [Lecture]. The Centre of New Fire, Ottawa.

Dissertation

UNPUBLISHED

Thompson, Kimberly J. (1992). *Continuity and change: Women's social participation.* Unpublished master's thesis, Cornell University, Ithaca, NY.

ABSTRACT

Shimko, Keith L. (1990). Images and policy debates (Doctoral dissertation, Indiana University, 1990). *Dissertation Abstracts International, 51A,* 1766 A.

Film

Costner, Kevin. (Director). (1990). *Dances with wolves* [Film]. Los Angeles: TIG/Orion.

Videocassette

Hamlet. (1987). [Videocassette]. London: BBC.

Radio/Television Programs

Blake, John. (Producer). (1986, May 10). Apartheid. In *Frontline*. Watertown, NY: WBNE.

Work of Art

Picasso, Pablo. (1912). *Still life with chair-caning* [Oil on canvas]. Musée Picasso, Paris.

Map

Physical United States. (1987). [Map]. Washington, DC: National Geographic Society.

Public Document

U.S. Department of State. (1948). *The Berlin crisis: A report on the Moscow discussions, 1948*. Washington, DC: U.S. Government Printing Office.

Manuscript

Hare, W.A. (1900). [Papers]. National Archives, Ottawa.

Computer

PROGRAM

Microsoft multimedia Beethoven: The ninth symphony [Computer software]. (1992). Redmond, WA: Microsoft Corporation.

ELECTRONIC DOCUMENT

Davis, R. (1993). [Review of the book *A question of leadership*]. *Australian Electronic Journal of History*, 1 (2), sec. 2. Available INTERNET: gopher to gopher.CIC.net, Electronic Serials Section

Indirect Sources

Pakenham, Thomas. (1979). *The Boer war*. London: Weidenfeld and Nicholson. Citing L. Curtis. (1951). *With Milner in South Africa* (87). Oxford: Oxford University Press.

Certain elements of these entries have been italicized. If you are writing with a word processor, use either italics or boldface for these elements. In handwritten or typed essays, elements italicized in these examples would be underlined. Two or more sources by the same author are listed in chronological order of publication. See Egerton in the sample *Works Consulted* on page 88.

An annotated bibliography requires making critical comments on the merits of each source.

Example:

Dunham, Aileen. (1963). *Political unrest in Upper Canada, 1815–1836.* Toronto: McLelland and Stewart.

> A detailed study of the underlying political events that led to the rebellion in Upper Canada in 1837. It is most useful for an understanding of the political problems of the period.

The list of sources for the League of Nations essay laid out in APA style is shown below.

WORKS CONSULTED

Barros, James. (1979). *Office without power.* Oxford: Clarendon Press.

Baer, George W. (1976). *Test case: Italy, Ethiopia, and the League of Nations.* Stanford: Hoover Institution Press.

Claude, I.L. (1981). Casual commitment to international relations. *Political Science Quarterly, 96,* 367–379.

Egerton, George W. (1978). *Great Britain and the creation of the League of Nations.* Chapel Hill, NC: University of North Carolina Press.

Egerton, George W. (1983). Collective security as political myth: Liberal internationalism and the League of Nations in politics and history. *International History Review, 5,* 496–524.

Kennedy, Paul. (1986). Appeasement. In Gordon Martel (Ed.), *The origins of the Second World War reconsidered: The A.J.P. Taylor debate after twenty-five years* (140–161). Boston: Allen and Unwin.

Northedge, F.S. (1986). *The League of Nations: Its life and times, 1920–1946.* Leicester: Leicester University Press.

Walters, F.P. (1952). *A history of the League of Nations.* Oxford: Oxford University Press.

CONCLUSION

Each essay is a journey of exploration and discovery. Like all journeys there will be both elation and tribulation, fascination and frustration. The excitement of probing problems and developing new insights will frequently be countered by difficulties of deadlines, finding sources, and crafting ideas into words. There is no "quick fix" formula for quality assignments. But with practice, patience, and enthusiasm you will be able to overcome the obstacles on your journey.

There is a method to researching and writing assignments in the humanities and social sciences, and the preparation of a good essay is not a mystery, as some students perceive it. This manual has outlined a method that follows a systematic and logical progression from the first step of selecting a topic through to the final submission of the completed assignment. You may wish to modify the method and shape your own process. No matter what method you develop, it is important to have a method for processing and communicating information and ideas.

In mastering the techniques of research and writing, you will have developed a valuable set of skills, cultivated important qualities, and derived a personal sense of satisfaction and achievement that creative activity can bring. Such talents can serve you well throughout life.

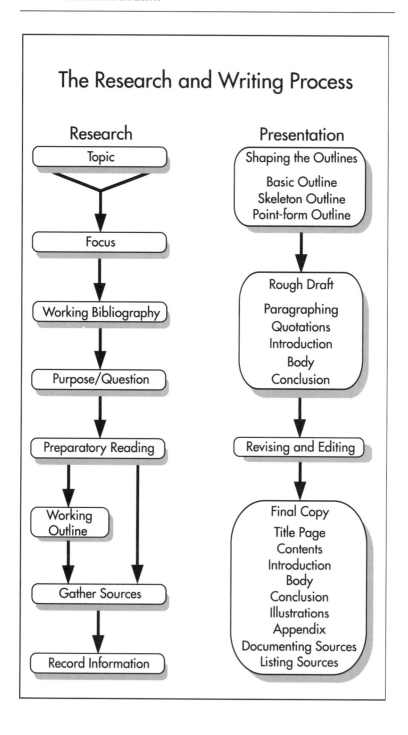

The Research and Writing Process

Research

- Topic
- Focus
- Working Bibliography
- Purpose/Question
- Preparatory Reading
- Working Outline
- Gather Sources
- Record Information

Presentation

- Shaping the Outlines
  - Basic Outline
  - Skeleton Outline
  - Point-form Outline
- Rough Draft
  - Paragraphing
  - Quotations
  - Introduction
  - Body
  - Conclusion
- Revising and Editing
- Final Copy
  - Title Page
  - Contents
  - Introduction
  - Body
  - Conclusion
  - Illustrations
  - Appendix
  - Documenting Sources
  - Listing Sources

APPENDIX

1. RESEARCH AIDS

• The resources that you should become acquainted with first are the catalogues of the libraries accessible to you. The library's catalogue is the main source of information about its books and other resources. It is usually the best place to start your search. Increasingly, libraries are replacing their card catalogues with databases of computer-readable records accessible through terminals. Read the "Help" screens carefully, and if you still have difficulties do not hesitate to approach the library staff for assistance. On-line computer catalogues offer greater versatility for searching than the traditional author/title and subject divisions of the card system. For example, in some systems you can search by a keyword in the title. Enter the term "imperialism" and the computer will list all works with "imperialism" in the title regardless of the position of the word. Consult library brochures and on-line help to explore the various searching options available through the catalogue.

• As mentioned above, keywords in titles can be useful in locating material on a subject. Since the richness of language usually permits a concept to be expressed in a number of different ways, it is possible that subject terms familiar to the researcher may not be the ones selected by the author for the title. To standardize terminology for searches so that material on the same subject can be found in the same place in the catalogue, the Library of Congress devised the *Library of Congress Subject Headings* (LCSH). If you look up the term "Diplomacy" in the LCSH, for example, you will find a number of related headings such as "treaties" and "summit meetings" that you can use in your search for sources. The list of subject headings in the LCSH is used widely in the catalogues of academic libraries and in some periodical indexes. There is also a *Canadian Subject Headings* for research related to Canadian topics.

● Although it may seem old-fashioned in the age of computer technology, browsing can be a very effective means of expanding your list of sources. You can locate your "browsing area" in the library by using the LCSH and the catalogue to determine which stacks hold books on your subject. By running your eye along the shelves you will often discover useful sources. And by checking tables of contents and indexes you will often pinpoint pertinent information in sources that would not be revealed in a catalogue search. A careful scrutiny of bibliographies and references in books on related topics will often turn up additional sources.

● The reference shelves, containing a wide assortment of material, can be an especially profitable area for browsing.

Atlases, e.g., *Atlas of Ancient Archaeology*
Almanacs, e.g., *The World Almanac and Book of Facts*
Yearbooks, e.g., *Urban History Yearbook*
Handbooks, e.g., *Handbook of Latin American Studies*
Research Guides, e.g., *Research Guide to Philosophy*
Chronologies, e.g., *World Chronology of Music History*
Dictionaries, e.g., *Dictionary of American Art*
Encyclopedias, e.g., *Encyclopedia of Crime and Justice*

Encyclopedias can be general such as the *Encyclopaedia Britannica* or specific such as *The Encyclopedia of American Foreign Policy*. You can gain access to hundreds of specialized encyclopedias by consulting *First Stop: The Master Index to Subject Encyclopedias*.

Many other interesting publications, such as the *World Treaty Index*, may be found on the reference shelves. There are published guides, classified by subject areas, that will assist you in determining the availability of reference material on your topic:

Guide to Reference Books
Walford's Guide to Reference Material
Guide to Reference Sources

All reference works in your library will be accessible through the main catalogue, but remember that reference material may not be removed from the library.

• Bibliographies are publications listing books, articles, and other sources on specific topics, and they can be accessed through the library's catalogue. They are especially useful because someone else has done the searching for you. Once published, however, they can become dated. On the other hand, many bibliographies are published annually. The following are a few of numerous bibliographies:

Africa Since 1914; A Historical Bibliography
Bibliographia Canadiana
International Geographical Bibliography

The *Bibliographic Index* is published three times a year, the third issue being the annual cumulation. It is a subject list of bibliographies published separately or appearing as part of books or articles.

• There is a time lag between the publication date and the cataloguing of books. Should you wish to identify books available commercially on your topic, but not held in your library, consult references such as:

Books in Print
Canadian Books in Print
Cumulative Book Index
Forthcoming Books
Whitaker's Books in Print

• Book reviews may enable you to determine the reliability of a book, and they will often provide additional information and insights on your subject. Consult references such as:

An Index to Book Reviews in the Humanities
Book Review Digest
Book Review Index
Book Review Index to Social Science Periodicals

Many periodical and newspaper indexes have sections on book reviews either under "Book Reviews," "Reviews," or in a separate section. Book reviews are useful if you are required to prepare a book report for one of your courses.

● Articles in scholarly journals and popular magazines are an excellent source of information because they are usually concise, specific, and current. Periodical indexes and abstracts are essential tools because they enable you to locate articles relevant to your subject in thousands of magazines and journals. The basic difference between abstracts and indexes is that the former not only index the articles but also summarize the subject matter. You might wish to start with the indexes and then move to the abstracts. The following are just a few that are useful for humanities and social science research:

> *Abstracts of Native Studies*
> *Environment Index*
> *Humanities Index*
> *Sociological Abstracts*

The *Essay and General Literature Index* is similar to a periodical index except that it provides access to essays in published anthologies. Some journals also publish their own specialized indexes, such as the *National Geographic Index, 1888–1988* and *Scientific American: Cumulative Index, 1978–1988*.

Citation indexes stand in a class of their own. Even though they can be used for a subject search, they really enable the researcher to identify related writings by indicating sources in which a known work by a given author has been cited. The *Arts and Humanities Citation Index* lists items from over 6000 of the world's leading journals and is published three times a year, the third issue being the annual cumulation. The *Social Sciences Citation Index* is also published three times a year with an annual cumulation, and it indexes items covering all disciplines in the social sciences in almost 5000 journals. Read the instructions that appear in the first volume of each index.

Periodical indexes can be either very specific, such as the *Music Index*, or general, such as the *Social Sciences Index*. When searching through the indexes and abstracts, it is advisable to peruse them systematically and sequentially year by year to avoid missing a volume. Some indexes start at the beginning of the century, while others are recent. It is even possible to delve into journals and magazines in the nineteenth century by using *Poole's Index to Periodical Literature* or *Wellesley's Index to Victorian Periodicals*. The needs of your assignment will determine whether you should use early or current periodicals.

Thousands of magazines and journals are published around the world each year. It is possible for you to determine which particular publications cover your subject area by consulting one of the following directories:

The Serials Directory
The Standard Periodicals Directory
Ulrich's International Periodicals Directory

These directories include more than just periodicals: * they also list newsletters, government publications, yearbooks, newspapers, and conference proceedings. The publications are classified by subject, and complete bibliographic details are usually provided, including where they are indexed. Some of these directories also provide a list of abstracts and indexes.

● Newspapers are a valuable source of information. The following are a sample of many newspaper indexes that will give you quick access to articles and editorials:

Canadian News Index (1977–1992)
Canadian Index (1993–) (also contains magazines and journals)
The New York Times Index
Index to the Times

The application of computer technology to the news industry has resulted in many newspapers developing electronic indexes such as the *New York Times* in *Nooz* and the *Globe and Mail's InfoGlobe*. There are also publications that provide lists of newspapers and indexes:

Checklist of Indexes to Canadian Newspapers
Gale Directory of Publications and Broadcast Media

---

* Periodicals comprise popular magazines and scholarly journals, whereas Serials, a broader category, covers periodicals as well as annual reports, yearbooks, newsletters, newspapers, and the proceedings of organizations.

● A number of publications provide annual reviews of developments in their disciplines or commentaries on publications published during the year. These include:

Annual Bulletin of Historical Literature
Annual Review of Energy
Annual Review of Jazz Studies
Film Review Annual

Additional review publications may be located in the serials and periodicals directories listed on the previous page.

● Biographical indexes are indispensable if you are studying an individual. These include:

American Women Writers
Biography and Genealogy Master Index
Biography Index
The Annual Obituary

● Masters theses and doctoral dissertations are useful for both content details as well as source information in their bibliographies. Consult indexes such as the following for university theses and dissertations on topics you are researching:

Canadian Theses
Dissertation Abstracts International
Index to Theses with Abstracts

● There are a number of publications that provide an analysis of current affairs. The back issues provide detailed digests of world news and public opinion over the past 50 years.

Editorials on File
Facts on File
Index to International Public Opinion
Keesing's Record of World Events

Current Contents is a weekly compilation of the tables of contents of hundreds of journals. The two sections of particular interest to social science and humanities students are *Social and Behavioral Sciences* and *Arts and Humanities*. Another source, *ABC Pol Sci*, reproduces tables of contents of 300 journals in politics and government.

• Many speeches, lectures, and presentations are delivered each year at conferences and conventions. Transcripts are often made available, and they are accessible through indexes such as the following:

Bibliographic Guide to Conference Publications
Directory of Published Proceedings
Index to Social Science and Humanities Proceedings
Proceedings in Print

• Vertical files containing newspaper clippings and pamphlets are kept in some libraries. These files are usually catalogued and contain a wealth of current information. There is also a *Vertical File Index.*

• Many publications are issued under the authority of governments around the world. A number of indexes are available to locate information in government publications such as the following:

CIS Index (U.S.)
Government of Canada Publications Catalogue
HMSO Monthly Catalogue (U.K.)
Index to International Statistics
UNDOC: Current Index: United Nations Documents

In some libraries, government documents are also accessible through the main catalogue.

• Much information is stored in microform today because of space limitations in libraries. Microfiche and microfilm are the two most common microforms. Material in microform includes out-of-print books, government documents, newspapers, periodicals, dissertations, pamphlets, indexes, and catalogues. There are a number of guides to this material such as the following:

An Index to Microform Collections
Microform Research Collections
Bibliographic Guide to Microform Publications
Subject Guide to Microforms in Print

● Computer technology is having a major impact on libraries and searching procedures.[*] Mention has been made of the on-line catalogue that is rapidly replacing the card catalogue. This system must not be confused with external database searching, which is often referred to as on-line reference.

Electronic networks are proliferating at a remarkable rate, and it is now possible to research databases around the world with ease and speed. While many networks are commercial operations charging fees, there are an increasing number of free networks available. Many educational institutions are already linked to networks, allowing not only access to databases but co-operative ventures between students around the world.

Electronic networks and databases are especially useful to searchers because:

◇ They permit speedy searching for sources in libraries, indexes, and abstracts.

◇ They may provide full text versions of newspapers, magazines, and encyclopedias.

◇ They allow access to statistical data such as weather information and stock prices.

Many organizations have also put their databases on compact discs known as CD-ROM, and these can be searched in the library, usually at no cost. Like external databases, CD-ROM versions have searching capabilities, full text sources, and statistical data. The CD-ROM version of a database is not as current as the on-line system but is nevertheless very useful and relatively easy to consult.

● This manual lists only English language titles because of space limitations. There are numerous works in other languages in each of the categories mentioned. If you do not read other languages, you can still gain access to other cultures and perspectives by reading works in translation. The *Index Translationum* and *Canadian Translations/Traductions Canadiennes* index translated books, while the *Translations Register-Index* lists unpublished translations into English.

---

[*] For a discussion of computer techniques and the more traditional searching methods, readers are encouraged to consult Thomas Mann's excellent publications listed in the bibliography of this manual.

● There is a wide range of non-print material available in the form of maps, statistics, photographs, taped interviews, films, television, radio, and computer programs. The following are just a few of numerous databases, indexes, and catalogues for films, videos, and television programs:

A-V Online
Bowker's Complete Video Directory
National Film Board of Canada Film and Video Catalogue
Watmedia Database

The *Media Review Digest* is an annual guide to reviews of non-book media.

Many libraries have special audio-visual rooms with catalogues and equipment. Holdings may include films, slides, filmstrips, records, compact discs, laser discs, and video and audio cassettes. Some libraries even permit overnight loans. Many libraries also have special map and atlas collections.

The current interest in oral history has resulted in many libraries and archives developing collections of audio-taped material. Refer to guides such as *Oral History Collections* and *Oral History: A Reference Guide and Annotated Bibliography* to determine the accessibility of oral material pertinent to your project. *Words On Cassette* is an extensive bibliography of material on audio-cassette. Consider interviewing and taping experts in your field or approaching eyewitnesses such as war veterans. Professors and teachers with special interests can also provide useful leads.

● Your library will not contain all existing publications, but an inter-library loan system facilitates obtaining material from other libraries. Computerized networks allow libraries to determine the location of a specific source quickly. Approach your librarian if you wish to use this service.

● Compile a list of museums, libraries, art galleries, and archives in your community.

2. THE WORKING OUTLINE

Sometimes it is possible to establish a tentative structure for the essay during the preparatory reading **before** you start recording information and ideas. As you read, jot down the possible factors around which you might structure an answer to your research question. For example, consider our question "Why did the League of Nations fail to maintain international stability in the 1930s?" As we worked our way through the preparatory reading, we would be looking for reasons *why* it failed to maintain international stability in the 1930s. List these reasons on a separate page headed Working Outline as shown below.

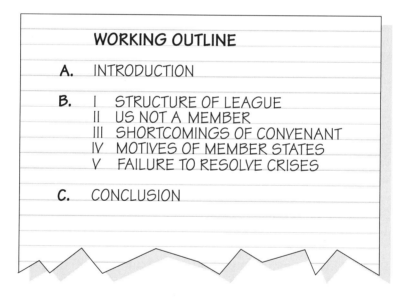

WORKING OUTLINE

A. INTRODUCTION

B. I   STRUCTURE OF LEAGUE
       II US NOT A MEMBER
       III SHORTCOMINGS OF CONVENANT
       IV MOTIVES OF MEMBER STATES
       V   FAILURE TO RESOLVE CRISES

C. CONCLUSION

List as many sections as you can in your Working Outline, but remember that they must be linked to the purpose of your research. **The research question shapes the contents of your Working Outline.** There is no special order and no magic number of sections in a Working Outline. List as many as you can, and then consolidate and reduce them if there are too many. From three to six sections should handle most questions comfortably.

You are researching and developing a response to your question — you are not simply writing a narrative chronicle, a descriptive account, or a biographical report. Ensure that your Working Outline does not lead you in the direction of one of the above. Chronological outlines, for example, can lead to narrative chronicles.

A Working Outline is not a straight-jacket that inhibits creativity because it is not a final plan for the essay. It is only a provisional structure to promote the clustering of ideas, insights, and information. The Working Outline is flexible — you may add sections during the research or you may delete some. Although developing a tentative structure will take more time initially, the time will be regained later because the outlining and drafting will be quicker. Furthermore, since the sections of the Working Outline are a direct response to the research question, they represent an emerging thesis or argument. However, a more immediate advantage of a Working Outline is having a framework for recording ideas and information.

The Working Outline can be used with either notepaper, index cards, or a computer to record information. Read carefully the research methods described on pages 17–28 because the information will not be repeated here.

Analysis is a detailed examination of your source material in accordance with the question or purpose of your essay. As we have shown, the research question (or purpose) shapes the structure of the Working Outline, which in turn provides the analytical framework for recording relevant ideas and information. In other words, the sections of the Working Outline provide the structure for collecting and classifying ideas and information.

If you prefer notepaper, allocate a separate page of notepaper to each section of the Working Outline as shown below. Read through your first source, for example the Northedge book coded LNLT, looking specifically for information relevant to your question. On page 51 there is reference to the ease with which states could join and leave the League. Since the problem of membership concerns the structure of the organization and "Structure of the League" is B. I on your Working Outline, write the note under B. I as shown below. Indicate the source code and page number in the left margin.

Continue reading through all your sources, searching for information and ideas relevant to your question, and then systematically record your notes under the appropriate section of the Working Outline as shown. When one section is full, head another page and continue recording your notes. You can use **both** sides of the page.

A.   INTRODUCTION

B.   I   STRUCTURE OF LEAGUE

LNLT
51
Only minimum qualifications needed to join the League. Could leave as easily as they joined.

If you prefer index cards, the method is similar to that described on pages 25–27. The only difference is that with a Working Outline you can assign a section number to each card as shown below. Each card will contain three items:

1. Source code and page;
2. Note;
3. Section number.

```
LNLT 51                              I

Only minimum qualifications needed
to join the League. Could leave as
easily as they joined



```

If you prefer using a computer, you can use index card software and set up the electronic cards as shown above. Or, you can use a word processor to create separate pages of electronic notepaper (or files) for each section of the Working Outline. You can then record the information in the appropriate file as shown on the previous page.

Sometimes a piece of information will not fit under one of the sections. You will either have to create another section in your Working Outline to incorporate the information, or you will have to discard the information as irrelevant to the essay. Do not create a Miscellaneous or General section because it will become a repository for inconsequential odds and ends and will soon dominate the other sections.

Once you have completed your research, your notes (on index cards, notepaper, or computer) will be grouped according to the sections of the Working Outline. It is difficult to write a final copy straight from these notes. A number of outlining and drafting stages will ensure a clear presentation of your answer. The first stage is primarily a name change. Once the research is finished, the Working Outline becomes the Basic Outline as shown below. It is possible that some of your sections may have to be deleted because of insufficient information. You will notice in our example that we have eliminated B. II US Not a Member and B. III Shortcomings of Covenant. These changes necessitated altering the numbering of the sections of the Basic Outline. The basic structure is now in place, though there may be a change in the order of the sections during the drafting.

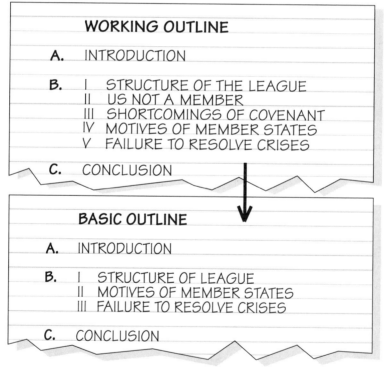

WORKING OUTLINE

A.   INTRODUCTION

B.   I   STRUCTURE OF THE LEAGUE
     II   US NOT A MEMBER
     III SHORTCOMINGS OF COVENANT
     IV   MOTIVES OF MEMBER STATES
     V   FAILURE TO RESOLVE CRISES

C.   CONCLUSION

BASIC OUTLINE

A.   INTRODUCTION

B.   I   STRUCTURE OF LEAGUE
     II   MOTIVES OF MEMBER STATES
     III FAILURE TO RESOLVE CRISES

C.   CONCLUSION

Continue now with the Skeleton Outline and the rest of the drafting process as explained on page 33.

3. ILLUSTRATIONS

There are two major types of illustrations: tables and figures. Tables contain statistical data, while figures consist of photographs, maps, drawings, graphs, diagrams, charts, and pictures. Software such as spreadsheets or graphics programs allow you to do most illustrations on computer. If computer facilities are not available, tables and figures can still be prepared by hand. Aim for clarity and simplicity when laying out your illustrations. Demonstrated in the following pages are some of the more commonly used illustrations.

Tables

Table 1. Population of Capital Cities, Selected Census Years				
CITY	1971	1976	1981	1986
St. John's, Nfld.	88 102	86 576	83 770	96 216
Charlottetown, P.E.I.	19 133	17 063	15 282	15 776
Halifax, N.S.	122 035	117 882	114 594	113 577
Fredericton, N.B.	24 254	45 248	43 723	44 352
Quebec, Que.	186 088	177 082	166 474	164 580
Toronto, Ont.	712 786	633 318	599 217	612 289
Winnipeg, Man.	246 246	560 874	564 473	594 551
Regina, Sask.	139 469	149 593	162 613	175 064
Edmonton, Alta.	438 152	461 361	532 246	573 982
Victoria, B.C.	61 761	62 551	64 379	66 303
Whitehorse, Y.T.	11 217	13 311	14 814	15 199
Yellowknife, N.W.T.	6 122	8 256	9 483	11 753
Ottawa, Ont.	302 341	304 462	295 163	300 763

Source: Data from *Canada Yearbook 1992* (Ottawa: Statistics Canada, 1991), 83.

Figures

Maps

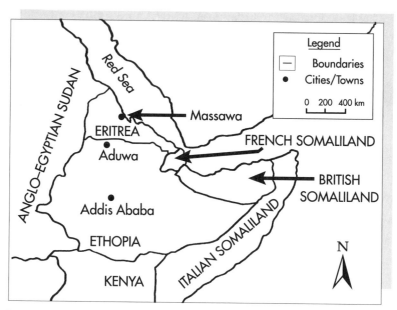

FIGURE 1. ETHIOPIA'S BORDERS, 1935.

Organizational Charts

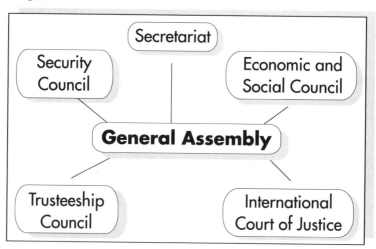

FIGURE 2. THE UNITED NATIONS SYSTEM.

Line Graphs

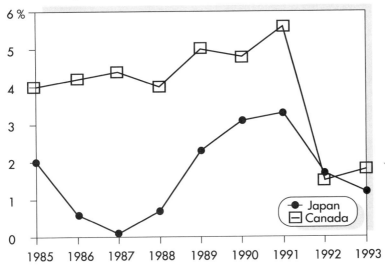

FIGURE 3. CONSUMER PRICES (ANNUAL PERCENT CHANGE).

Source: International Monetary Fund, *World Economic Outlook* (Washington, D.C.: International Monetary Fund, October 1993), 142.

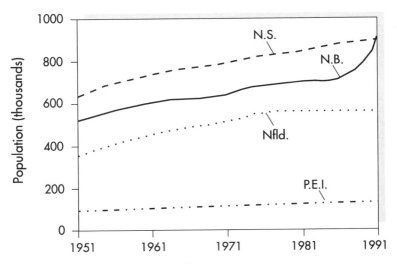

FIGURE 4. POPULATION OF ATLANTIC PROVINCES.

Source: John Robert Colombo, ed. *The Canadian Global Almanac 1994* (Toronto: Macmillan Canada, 1993), 42.

Bar/Column Charts

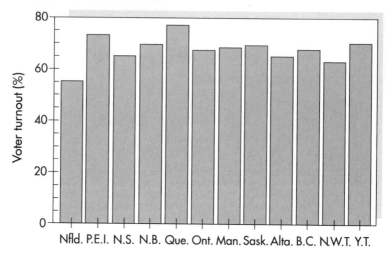

FIGURE 5. PERCENTAGE TURNOUT OF ELIGIBLE VOTERS BY PROVINCE IN THE 1993 FEDERAL ELECTION.

Source: Elections Canada, Ottawa.

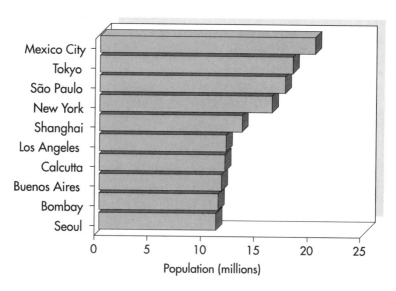

FIGURE 6. WORLD'S MOST POPULOUS CITIES, 1990.

Source: Robert Famighetti, ed. *The World Almanac and Book of Facts* (Mahwah, NJ: Funk and Wagnalls, 1993), 240.

Circle Charts

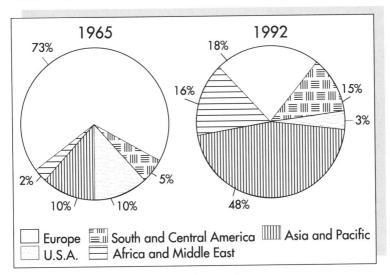

FIGURE 7. CANADIAN IMMIGRATION BY SOURCE AREA.

Source: Citizenship and Immigration Canada, *Annual Report to Parliament* (Ottawa, 1994), 15.

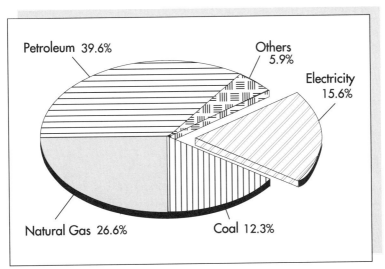

FIGURE 8. DOMESTIC DEMAND FOR PRIMARY ENERGY.

Source: Energy Statistics Handbook (Ottawa: Statistics Canada, 1994), 34.

4. THE ABSTRACT

An abstract forces the writer to examine closely the organization, argument, and presentation of the essay. It can also enhance the overall impression that your paper creates. It is written in concise essay form of between 100 and 300 words, and it is placed either on the title page or on the page immediately following. Ask your instructor whether an abstract is required and, if so, what the specific requirements are. The abstract is a short synopsis of the essay and, therefore, it must be written last. It must not be confused with the introduction with which there might, however, be some overlap. It may include all or some of the following features:

- Discussion of the topic and the selection of a specific problem or issue and its importance as a field for investigation.

- A clear statement of purpose or the research question.

- A statement of the thesis or argument and an explanation of the structure for the development of the thesis/argument.

- A definition of the limits of the assignment; a clarification of what is and is not being considered.

- A discussion of the various sources, primary and secondary, and their usefulness, as well as the bibliographic aids and libraries or archives used.

- The documentation system and the type of reference list, such as an annotated bibliography, for example, and whether explanatory notes have been used.

- A list of the contents of the appendix.

The question you should ask yourself is this: If the essay is lost and only the abstract survives, will it convey to the reader a clear picture of the essay, its central argument, and its organization?

5. EXAMINATIONS

Essays

Instructors frequently use the essay format when setting examinations, whether they are take-home examinations or examinations written under supervision. Essay-style examinations can measure a wide range of skills.

- Addressing and interpreting a question.

- Developing and substantiating an argument.

- The logical organization of ideas.

- Clear, precise expression.

- Critical judgement.

- Thinking clearly under time constraints.

These skills cannot be demonstrated in a knowledge vacuum: a sound grasp of the basic course material and the conceptual framework is essential. **Knowledge and skills are inseparable in the writing of good essay answers.** There are many similarities between the major term essay and the examination essay, though obviously the scale is different. The best practice for writing successful essay examinations is to develop and refine your research and writing skills during the course of the academic year.

- Discuss with your instructor:

    ❖ What will be covered and what will not be covered in the examination.

    ❖ What criteria will be used in assessing the answers.

    ❖ Whether the questions have to be answered in the order they appear on the examination paper.

    ❖ Whether you should double-space or single-space your writing

    ❖ Any other matters such as the use of the first person.

- Read the **entire** examination paper **slowly**.

  - Pay careful attention to the instructions and make sure you understand all the requirements.

  - Read the questions carefully, noting keywords such as "analyze" and "discuss."

  - Think carefully before selecting your questions (if a choice is permitted).

- Before you start writing:

  - Map out a schedule by allocating your time according to the marks awarded for each question. Allow time at the end for proofreading.

  - If you are permitted to answer the questions in any order, do those that you know best first.

  - Do not waste your time writing out the questions; just number your answers correctly.

- Preparing to write:

  - Decode keywords such as "trace" and "analyze" carefully. Misinterpreting important terms could be disastrous.

  - Address the question exactly as it is phrased. Do not side-step the question or substitute a title of your own creation.

  - Never change a question to suit a prepared answer.

  - Think carefully before tackling each question. Attempt a fresh interpretation.

  - Plan your answers carefully. Jot down relevant ideas and information and then arrange a basic ABC outline **before** you start writing.

  - Never write a rough draft and then a good copy. Plan and proofread your answers carefully to ensure neatness and accuracy.

- Writing the answer:
    - ✧ Keep the introduction short. Brief background information and a clear thesis statement (response to the question) is all that is needed for an examination introduction. Some instructors prefer just a statement of thesis and no background information.
    - ✧ Develop and substantiate your thesis/argument/answer/point of view in the body.
    - ✧ Complete your answer with a brief concluding paragraph in which you draw together the main threads of your answer and drive home your argument.
    - ✧ Use your ABC outline for each answer as a formula for shaping the paragraph structure. Avoid subheadings.
    - ✧ Write in a clear, crisp, and correct style. Precise, articulate expression has a persuasive power.
- The body is the most important part of an examination answer.
    - ✧ You have limited time so you must select just the essential and relevant information needed to support your answers.
    - ✧ Focus on your thesis and ensure that all the information is linked explicitly to it.
    - ✧ Convincing interpretations, judgements, and arguments have to be anchored in solid evidence and examples.
    - ✧ Illustrate and reinforce your answer with arguments from well-known authorities and sources where possible.
    - ✧ Avoid speculating and conjecturing about hypothetical situations.
    - ✧ Do not memorize quotations and then try to force them into your answers.

- Remember that examiners are busy people.

  ⬧ Developing a clear and convincing answer to each question is your sole task. Remember that the clarity of your answer is shaped largely by its structure and style.

  ⬧ Examiners are looking for incisive analysis and argument, not for chronological narrative and irrelevant description.

  ⬧ Remember the cliché: Quality not Quantity. It is true.

  ⬧ Write legibly. A paper that is easy to read will have a positive impact on the examiner. Avoid using correcting fluid and asterisks and arrows to make changes and additions.

  ⬧ Number your pages accurately.

- Watch the clock.

  ⬧ Follow the time schedule you mapped out at the beginning of the examination.

  ⬧ Allow time at the end to proofread your answers. Proofreading is fine-tuning, not major revising.

  ⬧ Complete the paper. Do not leave a scribbled list of points at the end with an apology to the examiner that you ran out of time. Examiners seldom accept that excuse because completing an examination within the time constraints is part of the test.

- Do not panic if you are confronted by a difficult paper. Scour the depths of your memory for all relevant information and plan an outline. You can probably squeeze through in a crisis with a moderate amount of knowledge, good organization, and polished writing skills. An attempt is better than no attempt at all.

Comparisons

Comparative questions are asked frequently in examinations. Unlike the single-focus essay, comparative questions require that you show the relationship (in the form of similarities and/or differences) between two individuals, ideas, or developments. **Comparisons are essays with a thesis or argument;** they are not descriptive narratives or biographical reports. Traditionally, "comparing" has meant focusing on similarities. But today, comparing is accepted widely as including similarities and differences. "Contrasting," however, means concentrating on differences only.

Let us assume that you have chosen the following comparative question in your final examination: "Compare and/or contrast the federal systems of government in the United States and in Canada." (When choosing comparative questions, ensure that you have a thorough understanding of **both** aspects or issues.) Allow more planning time for a comparative question and also reserve time at the end for proofreading. Since the structure of the comparative essay is more complex than that of the single focus essay, **you should not start writing your answer until you have planned the structure.** Your first step is to jot down the major similarities and differences in separate columns as shown in our example below.

Similarities	Differences
Federations	Senate
Passing legislation	Cabinet
Entrenched rights	Elections
Supreme Court	Powers
	Head of state
	Head of government
	Legislation
	Parties

Once you have identified the major similarities and differences you have to decide whether the similarities or the differences dominate the relationship. It is possible that the similarities and differences may be balanced evenly. Determining the extent of the similarities and differences is an important step because it will shape the thesis and the structure of the answer. In our example, there are more differences than similarities and, therefore, it is logical to focus the answer on the major differences between the federal systems of government in Canada and in the United States.

You cannot cover all the differences (or similarities) in an examination answer because of time constraints. Therefore, you have to be selective when setting up your Basic Outline and focus on the most important features of the relationship as shown in the example below.

BASIC OUTLINE

A.   INTRODUCTION

B.   I   ELECTIONS
     II   CABINET
     III LEGISLATION
     IV   SENATE

C.   CONCLUSION

The next step is to structure the Skeleton Outline showing the main supporting details for each major section. Remember that there must be corresponding examples and details (from both Canada and the United States in our example) to draw comparisons. **You cannot compare something with nothing**.

Once again the outlines will provide a formula for developing the paragraphs. In a shorter comparative examination essay (unlike the longer term paper), the Basic Outline establishes the paragraph structure, while the Skeleton Outline provides the supporting detail as shown in our example below.

SKELETON OUTLINE		
A.	INTRODUCTION 1. Brief background 2. Thesis statement	(paragraph)
B.	I ELECTIONS 1. Regular intervals/within 5 years 2. Senate, House of Reps./just Commons	(paragraph)
	II CABINET 1. Not in Congress/members of Commons 2. Legislation—influence differs	(paragraph)
	III LEGISLATION 1. Deadlocked/smoother passage 2. No fault in US/PM & cabinet responsible	(paragraph)
	IV SENATE 1. US elected/Canada appointed 2. Powerful/weaker	(paragraph)
C.	CONCLUSION	(paragraph)

Once the structure is mapped out with the supporting details, it is easy to start writing the answer following the advice provided earlier in this manual. It is important that you state the thesis concisely in the introduction (for example, "Although Canada and the United States have common characteristics, history has shaped two different and distinctive systems of government.") and that the body of the answer clearly demonstrates the links and the relationship stated in the thesis. You cannot expect the examiner to figure out the connections in a comparative answer. **Descriptive narrative is not comparative analysis**.

Glossary

Essay-style questions can be phrased in a variety of forms. Some questions may only require the presentation of information such as "Describe conditions in the Balkans in the spring of 1914." Other questions may require a point of view or argument, such as "How successful was Reconstruction after the American Civil War?" Questions requiring a response to a quotation are also common, such as "Assess the following comment: 'The League of Nations was primarily an organization for preserving the privileges of the major powers.'" The key word in each question will indicate the type of response required. Consult your instuctors about ambiguous terminology such as "analyze" and "discuss" **before the examinations**. Listed below are some of the more common terms used in examinations.

Assess: Examine and judge the strengths and weaknesses of an idea or argument and justify your conclusions.

Assess Paul Kennedy's explanation of the rise and fall of imperial powers.

Analyze: Identify and examine carefully the details and ideas and explain their relationship and/or demonstrate their importance.

Analyze the factors underlying US foreign policy in the 1930s.

Compare: Show the connection or relationship between different individuals, events, or issues by focusing on the similarities and/or differences.

Compare the federal systems of government in the United States and Canada.

Contrast: Show the connection or relationship between different individuals, events, or issues by focusing on the differences only.

Contrast the roles of the Canadian prime minister and the American president.

Sometimes both Compare and Contrast are used in a question.

Compare and contrast Canadian and American foreign policies in the Cold War era.
Compare and/or contrast the achievements of the League of Nations and the United Nations.

Criticize: Similar in requirements to *Assess*. *Criticize* does not mean focusing solely on weaknesses or negative aspects. Critical analysis is the detailed examination and assessment of an idea or passage.

Criticize Karl Marx's theory of surplus value.

Discuss: Examine an issue from all perspectives and present an argument with supporting evidence.

Discuss the role of missionaries in southern Africa in the nineteenth century.

Evaluate: Similar in requirements to *Assess* and *Criticize*. You may also be required to establish criteria for your evaluation.

Evaluate Durkheim's theory of deviance.

Explain: Examine and clarify an issue or idea.

Explain Mahatma Gandhi's philosophy of Satyagraha.

Some explanatory questions may require developing and substantiating a point of view.

Explain the failure of Alexander Kerensky's Provisional Government in 1917.

Interpret: Explain the meaning of a passage or quotation. The question usually also requires your assessment of the passage or quotation.

Interpret the following statement: Freedom is the prerequiste of great art.

Justify: Support an argument or position with evidence and reasons.

Justify US intervention in Grenada in 1983.

Refute: Oppose an argument or position with evidence and reasons.

Refute Brenton's contention that "there is a direct correlation between low taxes and violent crime in society."

Trace: Describe developments in narrative or logical order.

Trace the decline of the League of Nations.

ENDNOTES

1. Kate L. Turabian, *Student's Guide for Writing College Papers*, 3rd ed. (Chicago: University of Chicago Press, 1976), 31.

2. Harry F. Wolcott, *Writing up Qualitative Research*, Qualitative Research Methods Series, vol. 20 (Newbury Park, California: Sage Publications, 1990), 69.

3. Turabian, 26–30.

4. Alden Todd, *Finding Facts Fast* (Berkeley: Ten Speed Press, 1979), 10.

5. Edward de Bono, *CORT I: Teachers Notes* (New York: Pergamon, 1973), 7.

6. John M. Good, *The Shaping of Western Society* (New York: Holt, Rinehart, and Winston, 1968), 19.

7. R.J. Shafer, ed. *A Guide to Historical Method* (Homewood, Illinois: Dorsey Press, 1974), 101.

8. Sheridan Baker, *The Practical Stylist*, 7th ed. (New York: Harper and Row, 1990), 43.

9. William Zinsser, *On Writing Well*, 4th ed. (New York: Harper and Row, 1990), 3.

10. William E. Messenger and Jan de Bruyn, *The Canadian Writer's Handbook*, 2nd ed. (Scarborough, Ontario: Prentice-Hall, 1986), 241.

11. Zinsser, 7.

12. Gordon Taylor, *The Student's Writing Guide for the Arts and Social Sciences* (Melbourne: Cambridge University Press, 1989), 160.

13. Sylvan Barnet, *A Short Guide to Writing about Literature*, 6th ed. (New York: HarperCollins, 1992), 231.

14. Joseph Gibaldi and Walter S. Achtert, *MLA Handbook for Writers of Research Papers*, 3rd ed. (New York: MLA, 1988), 155.